GOD'S PROMISES AND BLESSINGS FOR AN ABUNDANT LIFE

With Biblical Prayers and God's Exhortations for
Life's Challenges

CHARLES MICHAEL

GIFTED BOOKS AND MEDIA

Copyright

Compiled by Charles Michael

Printed in the United States of America

Paperback ISBN: 978-1-947343-12-2

Published by Jayclad Publishing LLC
www.giftedbookstore.com

Table of Contents

12

Note to the Reader

How to Use this Book

God has hidden His promises and blessings in His Word and those who meditate and claim his Word are able to tap into God's hidden treasures which can elevate our life and give us the opportunity to live life the way He has intended it for us. The Psalmist begins his Psalm with these words, "Happy are those…" (Ps 1:1-6) and goes on to give the blessings one can receive by meditating on God's Word.

This book makes a sincere effort to bring out those promises and blessings and organizes it under various topics that are relevant to our times and need. The verses are put under five categories: namely , God's promises, God's blessings, Biblical prayers, God's advice, and God's warning. Every thought, word, and act of ours either pleases God or displeases God and likewise can either bring us a blessing or rob the God given blessing that were intended for us. If we are careful to obey all that the Word of God commands us to do , and moreover avoid all that the Word of God forbids us, then we will be blessed in every way.

Let us look at the type of verses included in this book which will give us knowledge about how to use each type of verse.

God's Blessings

Every commandment of God has blessings built into it. We inherit these blessings automatically when we obey that commandment or law of God. For example, we read in Ephesians, chapter 6, verse 1,

Children, obey your parents in the Lord, for this is just. Honor your father and your mother. This is the first commandment with a promise: so that it may be well with you, and so that you may have a long life upon the earth. (Eph 6:1-3)

The above verse gives a commandment and the blessing that go with it for those who obey and follow it. Obedience to parents, no matter how old you are, will bring wellness and long life with it. It is a God given spiritual law. Therefore every child who follows this commandment will be blessed and every child who violates this commandment will face the consequences of it. This book lists out the commandments and laws that God wants us to follow and the blessing that go with it.

God's promises

The second type of verses listed in this book are the promises of God. Promises of God are words spoken by God for the many challenges and situations that we face in life. Sickness, pain, job interviews, mortgage, financial debt, depression, mental illnesses, fear, worry, etc., are some common problems and challenges we face as part of this life. In times such as these, there are many voices that speak to us, some positive and some negative. God, in his infinite wisdom foresaw all these problems of man and has offered us a solution through the form of his Word. God's Word has the answers to life's needs and challenges. God's promises are words that speak to us directly in the situation that we are faced with. Instead of looking to the world for answers, we must look to God and find our comfort. For example, we read in the book of Deuteronomy,

> The LORD himself goes before you and will be with you; he will never leave you nor forsake you. Do not be afraid; do not be discouraged. (Deut 31:8)

It is a promise of God that can be claimed over many events of our life that calls for God's strength and support. If you are person afraid of driving or a new driver learning to drive, this verse is for you. The Word of God has the power to transform us and give us what it claims to give. All that we must do is read, repeat, meditate, and claim with faith and allow it to work within us.

God's advice

The third type of verses included in this book are the advice of God. A husband needs counsel and advice to keep his marriage happy and likewise a wife also needs advice. God, in his Word has given us everything we need to live a happy and joyful marriage. If we heed to God's advice, we will not only be happy and joyful, but also fulfill the call and purpose of our life.

God's warning

The verses listed under God's warning are sins that we must avoid to hold on to God's blessings. Every sin we commit has the power and potential to rob the God-given blessings.

Biblical Prayers

Lastly, this book also includes prayers that people have prayed during the biblical times which can be prayed by us for our various needs. Each time we pray with the words from scripture, we are meditating on God's word and unleashing its power in our lives.

Charles Michael

A

Abandonment

Prayer during times of abandonment
O God, my God, Why have you forsaken me? Why are you so far from helping me, and from the words of my groaning? My God, I cry out by day, and you will not heed, and by night, but find no rest. (Ps 22:2-3)

God's promise for those abandoned by parents and family
If my father and mother forsake me, then the Lord will take me up. (Ps 27:10)

I will not abandon you, and I will not neglect you. (Heb 13:5)

Remember these things, O Jacob, O Israel. For you are my servant. I have formed you. You are my servant, O Israel. You will not be forgotten by me. (Is 44:21)

Abortion (prolife)

God's warning for those who aid in abortion
For three wicked deeds of the sons of Ammon, and for four, I will not turn away the punishment, in so far as he has cut up the pregnant women of Gilead, so as to expand his limits. (Amos 1:13)

God's promise for the unborn
Your eyes did see my unformed substance; and in your book were written all the days that were made for me. (Ps 139:16)

God's promise for those who are prolife

God acted favorably toward the midwives. And the people increased, and they were strengthened exceedingly. And because the midwives feared God, he built houses for them. (Exo 1:20-21)

Addictions

Prayer for freedom from addictions

And now, what is it that awaits me? My hope is in you. Rescue me from all my iniquities. (Ps 39:7-8)

Prayer for freedom from drug addiction

O Lord, do not take your tender mercies far from me. Let Your mercy and your truth ever sustain me. For evils without number have surrounded me. My iniquities have taken hold of me, and I was not able to see. They have been multiplied beyond the hairs of my head. And my heart has forsaken me. (Ps 40:11-12)

Prayer for addicts (Deliverance from addictions)

May the groans of the shackled enter before you. According to the greatness of your arm, take possession of those doomed to die. (Ps 79:11)

God's promise for addicts

Sin will not have dominion over you. For you are not under the law, but under grace. (Rom 6:14)

All things are lawful to me, but all things are not beneficial: all things are lawful for me, but I will not be dominated under the power of anything. (1 Cor 6:12)

For freedom Christ has set us free. Stand firm, therefore, and do not submit again to a yoke of slavery. (Gal 5:1)

As far as the east is from the west, so far has he removed our iniquities from us. (Ps 103:12)

I am the Lord your God, who led you away from the land of the Egyptians, lest you serve them, and who broke the chains around your necks, so that you would walk upright. (Lev 26:13)

If the Son has set you free, then you will truly be free. (Jn 8:36)

God's promise of the Holy Spirit for victory over addictions
Not by might, nor by power, but in my spirit, says the Lord of hosts. (Zech 4:6)

Now the Spirit is Lord. And wherever the Spirit of the Lord is, there is liberty. (2 Cor 3:17)

Walk in the spirit, and you will not fulfill the desires of the flesh. (Gal 5:16)

You have not received a spirit of slavery to fall back into fear, but you have received the Spirit of adoption, in whom we cry out: "Abba, Father!" For the Spirit himself renders testimony to our spirit that we are children of God. (Rom 8:15-16)

Behold, I will kindle a fire in you, and I will burn up within you every green tree and every dry tree. The flame of the kindling will not be extinguished. (Eze 20:47)

Adultery

God's warning for those involved in adultery
Whoever is an adulterer, because of the emptiness of his heart, will destroy his own soul. He gathers shame and dishonor to himself, and his disgrace will not be wiped away. (Pro 6:32-33)

Adultery destroys marriage and family

You have taken his wife as a wife for yourself. And you have put him to death with the sword of the sons of Ammon. For this reason, the sword shall not withdraw from your house, even perpetually, because you have despised me, and you have taken the wife of Uriah the Hittite, so that she may be your wife.' (2 Sam 12:9-10)

Alcoholism

God's warning for those who are addicted to alcohol

For neither fornicators, nor idolaters, nor adulterers, nor the male prostitutes, nor sodomites, nor thieves, nor the greedy, nor the drunkards, nor slanderers, nor thieves shall inherit the kingdom of God. (1 Cor 6:9-10)

Do not gaze into wine when it turns gold, when its color shines in the glass. It enters pleasantly, but in the end, it will bite like a snake, and it will spread poison like a king of snakes. (Pro 23:31-32)

Almsgiving

What are the blessings we receive when we give alms and help the poor?

Our children and their descendants will be blessed

I have been young, and now I am old; and I have not seen the just forsaken, nor their children begging bread. They show compassion and lend, all day long, and their children will be in blessing. (Ps 37:25-26)

God will protect us and guard us from the evil one

Blessed is he who shows understanding toward the needy and the poor. The Lord will deliver him in the evil day. May the Lord preserve him and give him life, and make him blessed upon the earth. And may he not hand him over to the will of his adversaries.

May the Lord bring him help on his sickbed. In their illness you heal all their infirmities.(Ps 41:1-3)

God will keep us away from sin (darkness)
When you pour out your life for the hungry, and you satisfy the afflicted soul, then your light will rise up in darkness, and your darkness will be like the midday. (Is 58:10)

God will bless us in everything we do
Give liberally and without grieving when you give: because for on this account the Lord your God shall bless you in all your works, and in all that you put your hand into. (Deut 15:10)

God will bless us abundantly
Whoever is merciful to the poor lends to the Lord. And he will repay him for his efforts. (Pro 19:17)

Reach out your hand to the poor, so that your atonement and your blessing may be perfected. (Sir 7:32)

Give, and it will be given to you: a good measure, pressed down and shaken together and overflowing, they will place upon your lap. Certainly, the same measure that you use to measure out, will be used to measure back to you again. (Luk 6:38)

Pay attention to what you hear; the measure you give will be the measure you get, and still more will be given you. (Mrk 4:24)

Whoever is inclined to mercy shall be blessed, for from his bread he has given to the poor. (Pro 22:9)

Jesus, gazing at him, loved him, and he said to him: "One thing is lacking to you. Go, sell whatever you have, and give to the poor, and then you will have treasure in heaven. And come, follow me." (Mrk 10:21)

Do not be willing to forget good works and share what you have. Such sacrifices are pleasing to the Lord. (Heb 13:16)

We will receive an eternal reward
Sell what you possess, and give alms. Make for yourselves purses that will not wear out, a treasure that will not fall short, in heaven, where no thief approaches, and no moth corrupts. For where your treasure is, there will your heart be also. (Luk 12:33-34)

When you prepare a feast, call the poor, the disabled, the lame, and the blind. And you will be blessed because they do not have a way to repay you. So then, your recompense will be in the resurrection of the just. (Luk 14:13-14)

Ambitions and Goals

God's advice for our ambitions and goals
The mind of man plans his way. But it is for Lord to direct his steps. (Pro 16:9)

Let nothing be done by contention, nor from selfish ambition. Instead, in humility, let each of you esteem others to be better than yourselves. (Phil 2:3)

My thoughts are not your thoughts, and your ways are not my ways, says the Lord. For just as the heavens are exalted above the earth, so also are my ways exalted above your ways, and my thoughts above your thoughts. (Is 55:8-9)

Angels

God's promise of angelic protection around us

He shall give his angels charge over you, to keep you in all your ways. They shall bear you up in their hands, lest you dash your foot against a stone. (Ps 91:11-12)

The Angel of the Lord will encamp around those who fear him, and he will deliver them. (Ps 34:7)

My angel is with you, and he is watching over you. (Bar 6:7)

God's promise of Angelic help in our salvation

Are not all angels spirits in the divine service, sent to minister for the sake of those who shall receive the inheritance of salvation? (Heb 1:14)

Angelic protection for our journey

Behold, I will send my Angel, who will go before you, and preserve you on your journey, and lead you into the place that I have prepared. (Exo 23:20)

Anger

God's advice for those who get angry

Be angry, but do not sin. Do not let the sun set over your anger. Provide no room for the devil. (Eph 4:26-27)

Cease from anger, and forsake wrath: Do not fret; it brings only harm. (Ps 37:8)

Anger and fury are both abominable, and the sinful man will be held by them.(Sir 27:30)

Cease from anger, and leave rage; have no emulation to do evil. (Ps 37:8)

Ungodly anger can block blessings

You have heard that it was said to the ancients: 'You shall not murder; whoever will have murdered shall be liable to judgment.' But I say to you, that anyone who becomes angry with his brother or sister shall be liable to judgment. But whoever will have insulted his brother or sister shall be liable to the council. Then, whoever will have called him, 'you fool,' shall be liable to the fires of Hell. (Matt 5:21-22)

Anger of God

God's Word about His anger

For a brief moment, I have forsaken you, and with great pities, I will gather you. In a moment of indignation, I have hidden my face from you, for a little while. But with everlasting mercy, I have taken pity on you, said your Redeemer, the Lord. (Is 54:7-8)

Prayer to God for his mercy in times of his anger

You are a gracious God, and merciful, slow to anger, and of great kindness, and ready to forgive. (Jon 4:2)

Angry with God

I know your habitation, and your arrival, and your departure, and your madness against me. When you became angry against me, your arrogance rose up to my ears. Therefore, I will place a ring in your nose, and a bit between your lips. And I will turn you back on the road by which you arrived. (Is 37:28-29)

Anxiety

God's promise for those who are anxious

Be anxious about nothing. But in all things, with prayer and supplication, with acts of thanksgiving, let your petitions be made known to God. (Phil 4:6-7)

Blessed is the man who trusts in the Lord, for the Lord will be his confidence. And he will be like a tree planted beside waters, which sends out its roots to moist soil. And it will not fear when the heat arrives. And its leaves will be green. And in the time of drought, it will not be anxious, nor will it cease at any time to bear fruit. (Jer 17:7-8)

Cast all your anxiety upon him, for he takes care of you. (1 Pet 5:7)

God's Word about the dangers of anxiety

Envy and anger shorten life, and anxiety brings on old age before its time. (Sir 30:24)

Anxiety for wealth consumes the flesh, and thinking about it takes away sleep. (Sir 31:1)

Remove anxiety from your heart, and set aside pain from your body. For youth and pleasure are vain and empty. (Eccl 11:10)

Anxiety weighs down the heart, but a kind word cheers it up. (Pro 12:25)

Arrogance

God's warning for those who are arrogant

Talk no more so proudly; let not arrogance come out of your mouth: for the Lord is a God of knowledge, and by him actions are weighed. (1 Sam 2:3)

Arrogance precedes destruction. And the spirit is exalted before a fall. (Pro 16:18)

Arrogance is hateful in the sight of God and of men. And all iniquity among the nations is abominable. (Sir 10:7)

The one who secretly detracts his neighbor, I will destroy. The one with an arrogant eye and an insatiable heart, with that one I will not tolerate. (Ps 101:5)

Atheism (unbelief in God)

God's warning to atheists
The fool has said in his heart, "There is no God." They are corrupt, and they do abominable deeds. There is no one who does good; there is not even one. (Ps 14:1)

In the pride of their countenance the wicked say, "God will not seek it out"; all their thoughts are, "There is no God." His ways are stained at all times. Your judgments are removed from his face. He will be master of all his enemies. (Ps 10:4-5)

God's Word to claim over atheists
I will give them one heart. And I will put a new spirit within them. And I will take away the heart of stone from their flesh. And I will give them a heart of flesh. (Eze 11:19)

Attorneys (Lawyers, Advocates)

God's promise for attorneys
I have established you like a new threshing sledge, having serrated blades. You will thresh the mountains and crush them. And you will turn the hills into chaff. You will winnow them, and the wind will blow them away, and the whirlwind will scatter them. And you shall

exult in the Lord; you shall rejoice in the Holy One of Israel. (Is 41:15-16)

No weapon which has been formed to use against you will succeed. And every tongue that shall rise against you in judgment, you shall resist. (Is 54:17)

B

Baptism

What are the blessings we receive when we are baptized?

We become new creation

So if anyone is a new creation in Christ, what is old has passed away. Behold, all things have been made new. (2 Cor 5:17)

For in Christ Jesus, neither circumcision nor uncircumcision prevails in any way, but a new creation is everything! (Gal 6:15)

We are washed clean of our original sins

You have been washed, you have been sanctified, and you have been justified: all in the name of our Lord Jesus Christ and in the Spirit of our God. (1 Cor 6:11)

For you were darkness, in times past, but now you are light, in the Lord. So then, walk as children of the light. (Eph 5:8)

We are given the Holy Spirit

Indeed, in one Spirit, we were all baptized into one body, whether Jews or Gentiles, whether servant or free. And we all drank in the one Spirit. (1 Cor 12:13)

We begin the journey on the path of salvation

And now you also are saved, in a similar manner, by baptism, not by the testimony of sordid flesh, but by the examination of a good conscience in God, through the resurrection of Jesus Christ. (1 Pet 3:21)

He saved us, not by works of justice that we had done, but, in accord with his mercy, by the water of rebirth and by the renewal of the Holy Spirit. (Tit 3:5)

Whoever will have believed and been baptized will be saved. Yet truly, whoever will not have believed will be condemned. (Mrk 16:16)

We receive the promise of eternal life
You have been buried with him in baptism. In him also, you have risen again through faith, by the work of God, who raised him up from the dead. (Col 2:12)

Beatitudes

Blessed are the poor in spirit, for theirs is the kingdom of heaven.
Blessed are those who mourn, for they shall be consoled.
Blessed are the meek, for they shall inherit the earth.
Blessed are those who hunger and thirst for righteousness, for they shall be satisfied.
Blessed are the merciful, for they shall receive mercy.
Blessed are the pure in heart, for they shall see God.
Blessed are the peacemakers, for they shall be called children of God.
Blessed are those who endure persecution for the sake of righteousness, for theirs is the kingdom of heaven.
Blessed are you when they have reviled you, and persecuted you, and spoken all kinds of evil against you, falsely, for my sake:
Be glad and rejoice, for your reward in heaven is great. For so they persecuted the prophets who were before you. (Matt 5:1-12)

Bible (Word of God)

Prayer before reading the Bible

I am your servant. Give me understanding, so that I may know your decrees. (Ps 119:125)

I have rejoiced in the way of your commands, more than in all riches. I will meditate in your precepts, and examine your ways. I will delight myself in your statutes: I will not forget your word. (Ps 119:14-16)

Prayer after reading the Bible

Your word is a lamp to my feet and a light to my path. (Ps 119:105)

I rejoice at your word, as one that finds great spoil. I hate and abhor lying: but I love your law. (Ps 119:162-163)

I meditated on your commandments, which I loved. And I lifted up my hands to your commandments, which I loved. (Ps 119:47-48)

How have I loved your law, O Lord? It is my meditation all day long. (Ps 119:97)

I have acquired your decrees as an inheritance unto eternity, because they are the joy of my heart. I have inclined my heart to perform your statutes for eternity, as a recompense. (Ps 119:111-112)

I will rejoice over your words, like one who has found many spoils. (Ps 119:161)

Prayer of deliverance using God's Word

Rise up, O Lord, confront him and displace him. By your sword deliver my soul from the impious one. (Ps 17:13)

God's promise of the power of His Word

Heaven and earth shall pass away, but my words shall not pass away. (Matt 24:35)

The grass has dried up, and the flower has fallen. But the Word of our Lord remains for eternity. (Is 40:8)

All flesh is like the grass and all its glory is like the flower of the grass. The grass withers and its flower falls away. But the Word of the Lord endures for eternity. (1 Pet 1:24)

As rain and snow descend from heaven, and do not return there until they have soaked the earth, and watered it, and causing it to bloom and to provide seed to the sower and bread to the hungry, so also will my word be, which will go forth from my mouth. It will not return to me empty, but it will accomplish whatever I will, and it will prosper in the tasks for which I sent it. (Is 55:10-11)

Everyone who hears these words of mine and does them shall be compared to a wise man, who built his house upon the rock. And the rains descended, and the floods rose up, and the winds blew, and rushed upon that house, but it did not fall, for it was founded on the rock. (Matt 7:24-25)

God's promise for those who read the Bible out loud

Blessed is they that read aloud the words of the prophecy, and they that hear the words of this prophecy, and keep those things which are written in it. (Rev 1:3)

What are the blessings we receive when we read and meditate on the Word of God (Bible)?

General blessings

He who gazes upon the perfect law of liberty, and who remains in it, is not a forgetful hearer, but instead a doer of the work. He shall be blessed in what he does. (Jas 1:25)

God's Word fills our spiritual appetite

Man shall not live by bread alone, but by every word that proceeds from the mouth of God. (Matt 4:4)

God's Word can save us

Having cast away all uncleanness and an abundance of wickedness, receive with meekness the implanted Word, which is able to save your souls. (Jas 1:21)

I am not ashamed of the Gospel. For it is the power of God unto salvation for all believers, the Jew first, and the Greek. (Rom 1:16)

The Word of God breaks our hardness (Unbelief, Blocks, Obstacles)

Is not my word like fire, says the Lord, and like a hammer that breaks a rock in pieces? (Jer 23:29)

The Word of God can reach the innermost person and reveal us our inner nature

The Word of God is living and effective: more piercing than any two-edged sword, reaching to the division even between the soul and the spirit, even between the joints and the marrow, and so it discerns the thoughts and intentions of the heart. (Heb 4:12)

God's Word gives us direction and counsel

Your word is a lamp to my feet and a light to my path. (Ps 119:105)

Make my teaching your longing and desire, and you will be well instructed. (Wis 6:11)

God's Word teaches, reproofs, and corrects us

All Scripture, having been divinely inspired, is useful for teaching, for reproof, for correction, and for instruction in justice, so that the man of God may be perfect, having been trained for every good work. (2 Tim 3:16-17)

We receive emotional healing

The law of the Lord is perfect, reviving souls. The testimony of the Lord is faithful, providing wisdom to little ones; the justice of the Lord are right, rejoicing hearts; the precepts of the Lord is clear, enlightening the eyes. (Ps 19:7-8)

According to the multitude of my sorrows in my heart, your consolations have given joy to my soul. (Ps 94:19)

My soul has slumbered because of sorrow. Strengthen me in your words. (Ps 119:28)

I called to mind your ordinances of old, O Lord, and I was consoled. (Ps 119:52)

We are filled with the Holy Spirit

Give heed to my reproof. Lo, I will offer my spirit to you, and I will reveal my words to you. (Pro 1:23)

In him, you also, after you heard and believed the Word of truth, which is the Gospel of your salvation, were sealed with the promise of the Holy Spirit. (Eph 1:13)

We find freedom from sin and addictions

I will always keep your law, in this age and forever and ever. I shall walk at liberty, because I was seeking your commandments. (Ps 119:44-45)

Direct my steps according to your promise, and let no iniquity have dominion over me. (Ps 119:133)

I have hidden your word in my heart, so that I may not sin against you. (Ps 119:11)

How can young people keep their way pure? By keeping to your words. (Ps 119:9)

The mouth of the righteous speaks wisdom, and his tongue talks of justice. The law of his God is in his heart; none of his steps shall slip. (Ps 37:30-31)

I obtained understanding by your commandments. Because of this, I have hated every way of iniquity. (Ps 119:104)

When Asa had heard these particular words, and the prophecy of the prophet Azariah, the son of Oded, he was strengthened, and he took away the idols from the entire land of Judah, and from Benjamin, and from the cities that he had seized of mount Ephraim, and he dedicated the altar of the Lord, which was before the portico of the Lord. (2 Chron 15:8)

We receive direction and counsel in life
The book of this law shall not depart from your mouth. Instead, you shall meditate upon it, day and night, so that you may observe and do all the things that are written in it. Then you shall direct your way and understand it. (Josh 1:8)

Make my teaching your longing and desire, and you will be well instructed. (Wis 6:11)

God's promise of life when we read the Bible

This is the book of the commandments of God and of the law, which exists in eternity. All those who keep it will attain to life, but those who have forsaken it, to death. (Bar 4:1)

My son, guard my words and conceal my precepts within you. Son, preserve my commandments, and you shall live. And keep my law as the pupil of your eye. Bind it with your fingers; write it on the tablets of your heart. (Pro 7:1-3)

I will never forget your precepts: for by them you have kept me alive. (Ps 119:93)

If anyone will have kept my word, he will not see death for eternity. (Jn 8:51)

Holding to the Word of Life, until my glory in the day of Christ. For I have not run in vain, nor have I labored in vain. (Phil 2:16)

It is the Spirit who gives life. The flesh is useless. The words that I have spoken to you are spirit and life. (Jn 6:63)

God's Word fills us with hope

Whatever was written, was written to teach us, so that, through patience and the consolation of the Scriptures, we might have hope. (Rom 15:4)

If your law had not been my joy, then perhaps I would have perished in my misery. (Ps 119:92)

Remember your word to your servant, by which you have given me hope. This has consoled me in my humiliation, for your word has revived me. (Ps 119:49-50)

I rise before dawn and cry for help. For in your words, I have hoped beyond hope. My eyes preceded the dawn for you, so that I might meditate on your promise. (Ps 119:147-148)

God's Word increases our faith

Faith comes from what is heard, and what is heard comes through the word of Christ. (Rom 10:17)

Everyone who hears these words of mine and does them shall be compared to a wise man, who built his house upon the rock. And the rains descended, and the floods rose up, and the winds blew, and rushed upon that house, but it did not fall, for it was founded on the rock. (Matt 7:24-25)

God's Word fills us with joy

I discovered your words and I consumed them. And your word became to me as the gladness and joy of my heart. For your name has been invoked over me, O Lord, the God of hosts. (Jer 15:16)

This we write to you, so that you may rejoice, and so that your joy may be full. (1 Jn 1:4)

Tribulation and anguish have found me. Your commandments are my delight. (Ps 119:143)

If your law had not been my joy, then perhaps I would have perished in my misery. (Ps 119:92)

We grow in divine wisdom, knowledge, and understanding

The unfolding of your words illuminates, and it gives understanding to little ones. (Ps 119:130)

By your commandment, you have made me wiser than my enemies. For it is with me for eternity. I have understood beyond all my teachers. For your testimonies are my meditation. I have understood beyond the elders. For I have searched your commandments. (Ps 119:98-100)

Set your thoughts on the precepts of God, and be entirely constant in his commandments. And he himself will give you insight, and the desire of wisdom will be given to you. (Sir 6:37)

We receive healing
Indeed, neither an herb, nor a poultice, healed them, but your word, O Lord, which heals all. (Wis 16:12)

My child, pay attention to what I say, and incline your ear to my words. Let them not recede from your eyes. Keep them in the midst of your heart. For they are life to those who find them and health to all that is flesh. (Pro 4:20-22)

Material and spiritual blessings
Blessed is the man who has not followed the counsel of the wicked, and has not remained in the way of sinners, and has not sat in the chair of scoffers. But his will is with the law of the Lord, and he will meditate on his law, day and night. (Ps 1:1-2)

He who gazes upon the perfect law of liberty, and who remains in it, is not a forgetful hearer, but instead a doer of the work. He shall be blessed in what he does. (Jas 1:25)

God's promise of miracle and wonders for those read and meditate on his Word
By the word of the Lord, he closed the heavens, and he brought down fire from heaven three times. (Sir 48:3)

He raised up a dead man from the grave, from the fate of death, by the word of the Lord God. (Sir 48:5)

We receive financial blessings

The Lord your God will cause you to abound in all the works of your hands, in the progeny of your womb, and in the fruit of your cattle, in the fertility of your land, and with an abundance of all things. For the Lord will return, so that he may rejoice over you in all good things, just as he rejoiced in your fathers: but only if you will listen to the voice of the Lord your God, and keep his precepts and statues, which have been written in this law, and only if you return to the Lord your God with all your heart and with all your soul. (Deut 30:9-10)

Our prayers will be answered

If you abide in me, and my words abide in you, then you may ask for whatever you will, and it shall be done for you. (Jn 15:7)

Deliverance from evil

He sent his word, and healed them, and delivered them from their destructions. (Ps 107:20)

We are cleansed and purified when we read the Word of God

You are clean now, because of the word that I have spoken to you. (Jn 15:3)

Sanctify them in truth. Your word is truth. (Jn 17:17)

God's Word gives us truth about God and this life

If you will abide in my word, you will truly be my disciples. And you shall know the truth, and the truth shall set you free. (Jn 8:31-32)

The revealing of your words gives light; it gives understanding to the simple. (Ps 119:130)

God's Word fills us with peace

Those who love your law have great peace, and nothing can make them stumble. (Ps 119:165)

God's Word comforts us in our distress
This is my comfort in my distress: for your promises gives me life. (Ps 119:50)

Bitterness

God's Word about the dangers of bitterness
Let all bitterness and anger and indignation and outcry and blasphemy be taken away from you, along with all malice. And be kind and merciful to one another, forgiving one another, just as God has forgiven you in Christ. (Eph 4:31-32)

See to it that no one fails to obtain the grace of God, lest any root of bitterness spring up and impede you, and by it, many might be defiled. (Heb 12:15)

Blasphemy (Speaking against the LORD)

Prayer of repentance for speaking against the Lord
I have heard of you by the hearing of the ear: but now my eye sees you. Therefore I abhor myself, and repent in dust and ashes. (Job 42:5-6)

God's warning for those who blaspheme
Jerusalem is ruined, and Judah has fallen, because their words and their plans are against the Lord, in order to provoke the eyes of his majesty. (Is 3:8)

Blessing Prayers

Blessing prayer over families

May the Lord add blessings upon you: upon you, and upon your children. May you be blessed by the Lord, who made heaven and earth. (Ps 115:14-15)

Blessing prayer over people who seek our blessings

May he grant to you according to your heart's desires, and fulfill all your plans. We will rejoice in your salvation, and in the name of our God, we will be magnified. May the Lord fulfill all your petitions. (Ps 20:4-5)

Blessing prayer for graduation, marriage, etc.

May God almighty bless you, and may he cause you to increase and also to multiply, so that you may be influential among the people. (Gen 28:3)

Blessing prayer on Birthdays

May the Lord bless you and keep you. May the Lord make his face to shine on you and be gracious on you. May the Lord turn his countenance toward you and grant peace to you. (Num 6:24-26)

Blessing prayer on newly weds

Blessed shall you be in the city, and blessed in the field. Blessed shall be the fruit of your womb, and the fruit of your land, and the fruit of your cattle, the droves of your herds, and the folds of your sheep. Blessed shall be your barns, and blessed your storehouses. Blessed shall you be when you come in and when you go out. (Deut 28:2-6)

Blessing prayer over congregation

The grace of our Lord Jesus Christ, and the love of God, and the communion of the Holy Spirit be with you all. Amen. (2 Cor 13:13)

Grace to you, and peace, from God our Father and from the Lord Jesus Christ. (Rom 1:7)

May the Lord of peace himself give you an everlasting peace, in all ways. May the Lord be with all of you. (2 Thes 3:16)

May the grace of our Lord Jesus Christ be with you all. (2 Thes 3:18)

Blessing prayer of healing and wellness over others
Beloved, concerning everything, I make it my prayer that all may go well with you and that you may be in good health as with your soul. (3 Jn 1:2)

Blessing prayer for help received
May you be blessed by the Lord for you have shown me compassion. (1 Sam 23:21)

Blessing prayer over someone who is undergoing suffering
May you be made strong with all the strength that comes from his glorious power, and may you be prepared to endure everything with patience, while joyfully giving thanks to the Father, who has enabled you to share in the inheritance of the saints in the light. (Col 1:11-12, NRSVCE)

Blessing prayer over employees, servants, maids
The Lord will send forth a blessing upon your cellars, and upon all the works of your hands. And he will bless you in the land that you shall receive. (Deut 28:8)

Blessing prayer over someone for prosperity
I make it my prayer that all may go well with you and that you may be in good health, just as it with your soul. (3 Jn 1:2)

Blessing prayer of peace
Peace, peace to you, and peace to your helpers. For your God helps you. (1 Chron 12:18)

Blessing prayer over leaders

May the Lord give you prudence and understanding, so that you may be able to rule and to guard the law of the Lord your God. For then you will be able to prosper, if you keep the commandments and judgments that the Lord instructed. Be strong and of good courage. You should not fear, and you should not dread. (1 Chron 22:12-13)

Blessing prayer over businesses

May the Lord, the God of your fathers, add to this number many thousands more, and may he bless you, just as he has said. (Deut 1:11)

Blessing of parents for children who are leaving home for college or job

The Lord will guard you from all evil. He will guard your life. The Lord will guard your entrance and your exit, from this time and forevermore. (Ps 121:7-8)

Blocks (obstacles to blessings)

God's promise for the various blocks and hinderances we experience

I will go before you. And I will level the mountains. I will shatter the doors of bronze, and I will break apart the bars of iron. I will give you the treasures of darkness, and hidden riches of secret places, so that you may know that I am the Lord, the God of Israel, who calls your name. (Is 45:2-3)

What are the main blocks to our blessings?

Unbelief (Lack of faith)

He was not able to perform any miracles there, except that he cured a few of the infirm by laying his hands on them. And he wondered, because of their unbelief, and he traveled around in the villages, teaching. (Mrk 6:5-6)

Unforgiveness

A man holds on to anger against another man, and does he then expect healing from God? (Sir 28:3)

Sin

Behold, the hand of the Lord has not been shortened, so that it cannot save, and his ear has not been blocked, so that it cannot hear. But your iniquities have made a division between you and your God, and your sins have concealed his face from you, so that he would not hear. (Is 59:1-2)

Occult activities

The soul who will have turned aside to astrologers and soothsayers, and who will have fornicated with them, I will set my face against him, and I will destroy him from the midst of his people. (Lev 20:6)

Blood of Jesus

What are the blessing we receive by washing and covering ourselves in the Blood of Jesus?

We can Overcome Satan and his tactics

They overcame him by the blood of the Lamb and by the word of his testimony. And they loved not their own lives, even unto death. (Rev 12:11)

We attain redemption

For you know that it was not with corruptible gold or silver that you were redeemed away from your useless behavior in the traditions of your fathers, but it was with the precious blood of Christ, an immaculate and undefiled lamb. (1 Pet 1:18-19)

In him, we have redemption through his blood: the remission of sins in accord with the riches of his grace. (Eph 1:7)

We are cleansed from our sin (unrighteousness)

If the blood of goats and oxen, and the ashes of a calf, when these are sprinkled, sanctify those who have been defiled, in order to cleanse the flesh, how much more will the blood of Christ, who through the eternal Spirit has offered himself, immaculate, to God, cleanse our conscience from dead works, in order to serve the living God? (Heb 9:13-14)

Blessed are those who wash their robes in the blood of the Lamb. So may they have a right to the tree of life; so may they enter through the gates into the City. (Rev 22:14)

If we walk in the light, just as he also is in the light, then we have fellowship with one another, and the blood of Jesus Christ, his Son, cleanses us from all sin. (1 Jn 1:7)

The bodies of those animals whose blood is carried into the Holy of holies by the high priest, on behalf of sin, are burned outside the camp. Because of this, Jesus, too, in order to sanctify the people by his own blood, suffered outside the gate. (Heb 13:11-12)

Our sins are forgiven

For this is my blood of the new covenant, which shall be shed for many as a remission of sins. (Matt 26:28)

Nearly everything, according to the law, is to be cleansed with blood. And without the shedding of blood, there is no forgiveness of sins. (Heb 9:22)

God enters into covenant with us

Taking the chalice, he gave thanks. And he gave it to them, saying: "Drink from this, all of you. For this is my blood of the new covenant, which shall be shed for many as a remission of sins. (Matt 26:27-28)

Taking up the blood, he sprinkled it on the people, and he said, "This is the blood of the covenant, which the Lord has formed with you concerning all these words." (Exo 24:8)

We get freedom from sins
Grace to you and peace from him who is and who was and who is to come, and from the seven spirits who are before his throne, and from Jesus Christ, the faithful witness, the firstborn of the dead, and the ruler of the kings of the earth. To him who loves us and freed us from our sins by his blood. (Rev 1:4-5)

We are atoned
The life of the flesh is in the blood, and I have given it to you, so that you may atone with it upon the altar for your souls, and so that the blood may be for an expiation of the soul.(Lev 17:11)

We have been justified freely by his grace through the redemption that is in Christ Jesus, whom God has offered as a sacrifice of atonement, through faith in his blood, to reveal his justice for the remission of the former sins. (Rom 3:24-25)

We are justified
Christ died for us. Therefore, having been justified now by his blood, all the more so shall we be saved from wrath through him. (Rom 5:9)

We are protected
The Lord will cross through, striking the Egyptians. And when he will see the blood on the upper threshold, and on both the door posts, he will pass over the door of the house and not permit the Striker to enter into your houses or to do harm. (Exo 12:23)

The blood will be for you as a sign in the buildings where you will be. And I will see the blood, and I will pass over you. And the plague will not be with you to destroy, when I strike the land of Egypt. (Exo 12:13)

We are made worthy to come before God's presence
So, brothers, have faith in the entrance into the Holy of Holies by the blood of Christ, and in the new and living Way, which he has initiated for us by the veil, that is, by his flesh, and in the Great Priest over the house of God. (Heb 10:19-21)

Boasting

God's word about the dangers of boasting
What do you have that you have not received? But if you have received it, why do you boast, as if you had not received it? (1 Cor 4:7)

It is not good for you to boast. Do you not know that a little leaven corrupts the entire mass? Purge the old leaven, so that you may become the new bread, for you are unleavened. (1 Cor 5:7)

What is your life? It is a mist that appears for a brief time, and afterwards will vanish away. So what you ought to say is: "If the Lord wills," or, "If we live," we will do this or that. But now you exult in your arrogance. All such boasting is wicked. (Jas 4:15-16)

Body

God's promise for our body
Our way of life is in heaven. And from heaven, too, we await the Savior, our Lord Jesus Christ, who will transform the body of our lowliness, according to the form of the body of his glory, by means of that power by which he is even able to subject all things to himself. (Phil 3:20-21)

God's Word about the purpose of our body
Do you not know that your bodies are the Temple of the Holy Spirit, who is in you, whom you have from God, and that you are not your

own? For you have been bought at a great price. Glorify and carry God in your body. (1 Cor 6:19-20)

God's warning to those who sin in the body
Do you not know that you are the Temple of God, and that the Spirit of God lives within you? But if anyone violates the Temple of God, God will destroy him. For the Temple of God is holy, and you are that Temple. (1 Cor 3:16-17)

Born Again

What are the blessings of being born again (born in the spirit)?
A born again person will not sin
We know that everyone who is born of God does not sin. Instead, the one who was born of God protects him, and the evil one cannot touch him. (1 Jn 5:18)

We enter the kingdom of God
Amen, amen, I say to you, unless one has been born by water and Spirit, he is not able to enter into the kingdom of God. (Jn 3:5)

Amen, amen, I say to you, unless one has been reborn anew, he is not able to see the kingdom of God. (Jn 3:3)

Bribe

God's warning to those who give and receive bribe
Whoever pursues unjust gain disturbs his own house. But whoever hates bribes shall live. (Pro 15:27)

Neither shall you accept bribes, which blind even the prudent and subvert the words of the just. (Exo 23:8)

You shall not accept a person's reputation, nor bribe. For bribe blind the eyes of the wise and alter the words of the just. (Deut 16:19)

Brokenhearted (Heartbroken)

God's promise for the Heartbroken

He heals the brokenhearted and binds up their wounds. (Ps 147:3)

The Lord is near to those who are troubled in heart, and he will save the crushed in spirit. (Ps 34:18)

Be glad and rejoice together! For the Lord has consoled his people. He has redeemed Jerusalem. (Is 52:9)

Business Owners

God's advice to business owners

Do not choose to be anxious for dishonest wealth. For these things will not benefit you in the day of darkness and retribution. (Sir 5:8)

Whoever pursues unjust gain disturbs his own house. (Pro 15:27)

Two kinds of things have seemed difficult and dangerous to me: a merchant will not be easily freed from his negligence, and a shopkeeper will not be justified by the sins of his lips. (Sir 26:29)

The bread of lies is sweet to a man. But afterwards, his mouth will be filled with pebbles. (Pro 20:17)

When you make a sale to your neighbor or buy from your fellow citizen, you shall not cheat one another. (Lev 25:14)

C

Call

God's promise about our call

Before I formed you in the womb, I knew you. And before you went forth from the womb, I sanctified you. And I made you a prophet to the nations. (Jer 1:5)

The Lord has called me from the womb; from the womb of my mother, he has been mindful of my name. And he has appointed my mouth as a sharp sword. In the shadow of his hand, he has protected me. And he has appointed me as an elect arrow. In his quiver, he has hidden me. (Is 49:1-2)

But, when it pleased him who, from my mother's womb, had set me apart, and who has called me by his grace, to reveal his Son within me, so that I might evangelize him among the Gentiles. (Gal 1:15-16)

Blessed be the God and Father of our Lord Jesus Christ, who has blessed us with every spiritual blessing in the heavens, in Christ, just as he chose us in him before the foundation of the world, so that we would be holy and blameless in his sight, in love. (Eph 1:3-4)

Car (Vehicle)

God's promise for our vehicle and protection while driving

I will be to it a wall of fire all around, says the Lord, and I will be the glory within it. (Zech 2:5)

Career

God's promise for our career and future

I will instruct you and teach you in the way which you should go: I will guide you with my eyes upon you. (Ps 32:8)

Trust in the Lord with all your heart, and do not depend upon your own insight. In all your ways, acknowledge him, and he himself will direct your steps. (Pro 3:5-6)

Delight in the Lord, and he will grant to you the desires of your heart. (Ps 37:4)

I know the plans that I have for you, says the Lord, plans of your welfare, and not for evil, to give you a future of hope. (Jer 29:11)

Thus says the Lord, your Redeemer, the Holy One of Israel: I am the Lord, your God, who teaches you for your own good, who guides you in the way that you should go. (Is 48:17)

Charisms of the Holy Spirit

God's promise of the Charisms of the Holy Spirit

However, the manifestation of the Spirit is given to each one toward what is beneficial. Certainly, to one, through the Spirit, is given words of wisdom; but to another, according to the same Spirit, words of knowledge; to another, in the same Spirit, faith; to another, in the one Spirit, the gift of healing; to another, miraculous works; to another, prophecy; to another, the discernment of spirits; to another, different kinds of tongues; to another, the interpretation of tongues. (1 Cor 12:7-10)

Cheating

God's warning to those who cheat

Woe to one who builds his house with injustice and his upper rooms without judgment, who oppresses his friend without cause and does not pay him his wages. (Jer 22:13)

When you make a sale to your neighbor or buy from your fellow citizen, you shall not cheat one another. (Lev 25:14)

You should not harm the servant whose works are honest, nor the hired hand who entrusts his life to you. Let an understanding servant be loved by you like your own soul. You should not cheat him out of freedom, nor abandon him to destitution. (Sir 7:20-21)

Children

God's promise for our children

Behold, your children approach, whom you sent away scattered. They approach, gathering together, from the east all the way to the west, at the word of the Holy One, rejoicing in the honor of God. (Bar 4:37)

Arise, O Jerusalem, and stand in exaltation, and look around towards the east, and see your children, gathering together, from east to west, by the word of the Holy One, rejoicing that they are remembered by God. For they went out from you on foot, led by the enemies, but the Lord will lead them to you, being carried in honor like sons of the kingdom. (Bar 5:5-6)

God's promise for our children who are lost to sin, addictions, and unbelief

I will strengthen the house of Judah, and I will save the house of Joseph, and I will convert them, because I will have mercy on them.

And they will be as they were when I had not cast them away. For I am the Lord their God, and I will hear them. (Zech 10:6)

God's promise of the Holy Spirit upon our children
I will pour out waters upon the thirsty ground, and rivers upon the dry land. I will pour out my Spirit upon your descendants, and my blessing upon your offspring. (Is 44:3)

This is my covenant with them, says the Lord. My Spirit is within you, and my words, which I have put in your mouth, will not withdraw from your mouth, nor from the mouth of your offspring, nor from the mouth of your offspring's offspring, says the Lord, from this moment, and even forever. (Is 59:21)

God's promise for those whose children are away from the Lord
They will return from the land of the enemy. And there is hope for your very end, says the Lord. And your children will return to their own land. (Jer 31:16-17)

Fear not, for I am with you. I will bring your offspring from the East, and I will gather you from the West. (Is 43:5)

Lift up your eyes all around and see! All these have been gathered together; they have arrived before you. Your sons will arrive from far away, and your daughters will rise up from your side. Then you will see, and you will be radiant, and your heart will rejoice and be amazed. (Is 60:4-5)

What are the blessings that children receive when they obey and honor their parents?
Long life and wellness
Children, obey your parents in the Lord, for this is just. Honor your father and your mother. This is the first commandment with a

promise: so that it may be well with you, and so that you may have a long life upon the earth. (Eph 6:1-3)

Honor your father and your mother, so that you may have a long life upon the land, which the Lord your God will give to you. (Exo 20:12)

He who honors his father will live a long life. (Sir 3:6)

Atonement for sins
Those who honor their father atone for sins. And, like one who stores up treasure, so also is he who honors his mother. (Sir 3:3-4)

Kindness to a father will not be forgotten, and will be credited to you against your sins; in the day of your distress it will be remembered in your favor; like frost in fair weather, your sins will melt away. (Sir 3:14-15)

Graces and favors from God
The glory of a man is from the honor of his father, and a father without honor is a discredit to the son. (Sir 3:11)

Listen, my son, to the discipline of your father, and forsake not the law of your mother, so that grace may be added to your head and a collar to your neck. (Pro 1:8-9)

Obedience to parents pleases God
Children, obey your parents in all things. For this is well-pleasing to the Lord. (Col 3:20)

Salvation
Listen to the judgment of your father, and act accordingly, so that you may be saved. (Sir 3:2)

Wisdom and prudence in a person's life
Listen, children, to the discipline of a father, and pay attention, so that you may know prudence. (Pro 4:1)

Family blessings
The blessing of the father strengthens the houses of the children; but the curse of the mother uproots even its foundation. (Sir 3:9)

Childless couples, Barrenness

God's promise to childless couples for the gift of a child
He gives the barren woman to live in a house, makes her the joyful mother of children. (Ps 113:9)

If, after you have heard these ordinances, you keep and do them, the Lord your God will also keep his covenant with you and the mercy that he swore to your fathers. And he will love you and multiply you. And he will bless the fruit of your womb, and the fruit of your land: your grain as well as your vintage, oil, and herds, and the flocks of your sheep, upon the land about which he swore to your fathers that he would give it to you. (Deut 7:12-13)

You shall worship the Lord your God, so that I may bless your bread and your waters, and so that I may take away sickness from your midst. There will not be fruitless or barren ones in your land. I will fill up the number of your days. (Exo 23:25-26)

Children of God

What are the promises for being a child of God?
We can call God "our Father"
Therefore, you shall pray in this way: Our Father, who is in heaven: May your name be kept holy. (Matt 6:9)

We can receive the Holy Spirit
Therefore, because you are children, God has sent the Spirit of his Son into your hearts, crying out: "Abba, Father." (Gal 4:6)

We have an eternal inheritance

He has predestined us to adoption as children, through Jesus Christ, in himself, according to the purpose of his will, for the praise of the glory of his grace, with which he has gifted us in his beloved Son. (Eph 1:5-6)

When the fullness of time arrived, God sent his Son, formed from a woman, formed under the law, so that he might redeem those who were under the law, in order that we might receive adoption as children. (Gal 4:4-5)

We will be disciplined and pruned by God

Recognize then in your heart that, just as a parent disciplines his child, so has the Lord your God disciplined you. (Deut 8:5)

Persevere in discipline. God presents you to himself as children. But what child is there, whom his father does not correct? (Heb 12:7)

Christians

Prayer for Christians

O Lord God, do not destroy your people and your inheritance, whom you have redeemed in your greatness, whom you have led away from Egypt with a strong hand. (Deut 9:26)

Church

God's promise for the Church

In the last days, the mountain of the house of the Lord will be prepared at the summit of the mountains, and it will be exalted above the hills, and all the nations shall flow to it. (Is 2:1)

I say to you, that you are Peter, and upon this rock I will build my Church, and the gates of Hell shall not prevail against it. (Matt 16:18)

He has subjected all things under his feet, and he has made him the head over the entire Church, which is his body and which is the fullness of him who accomplishes everything in everyone. (Eph 1:22-23)

I will give you the keys of the kingdom of heaven. And whatever you shall bind on earth shall be bound, even in heaven. And whatever you shall release on earth shall be released, even in heaven. (Matt 16:19)

Whoever receives you, receives me. And whoever receives me, receives him who sent me. (Matt 10:40)

Whoever listens to you, listens to me. And whoever rejects you, rejects me. And whoever rejects me, rejects him who sent me. (Luk 10:16)

Calling together the twelve Apostles, he gave them power and authority over all demons and to cure diseases. And he sent them to preach the kingdom of God and to heal the sick. (Luk 9:1)

I will lead them to my holy mountain, and I will gladden them in my house of prayer. Their burnt offerings and their victims will be pleasing to me upon my altar. For my house will be called the house of prayer for all peoples. (Is 56:7)

Blessing prayer over one overseeing the building of a new Church
Be strong and of good courage, and carry it out. You should not be afraid, and you should not be dismayed. For the Lord my God will be with you, and he will not send you away, nor will he abandon you, until you have finished the entire work for the service of the house of the Lord. (1 Chron 28:20)

Cleanliness

Whether you eat or drink, or whatever else you may do, do everything for the glory of God. (1 Cor 10:31)

Clothes (grooming, makeup)

God's advice for those who are preoccupied about what to wear or how they look

Why do you worry about clothing? Consider the lilies of the field, how they grow; they neither work nor weave. But I say to you, that not even Solomon, in all his glory, was clothed like one of these. So if God so clothes the grass of the field, which is here today, and cast into the oven tomorrow, how much more will clothe you, O little in faith? (Matt 6:28-30)

For you, there should be no unnecessary adornment of the hair, or wearing gold, or the wearing of ornate clothing. Instead, your adornment should be of the inner self, with the incorruptibility of a quiet and meek spirit, which is precious in the sight of God. (1 Pet 3:3-4)

Commandments

What are the blessings we receive when we obey the commandments?

God's mercy

You shall know that the Lord your God himself is a strong and faithful God, preserving his covenant and his mercy for those who love him and those who keep his commandments for a thousand generations. (Deut 7:9)

Eternal reward

Whoever despises the word bring destruction on himself. but those who respect the commandment shall be rewarded. (Pro 13:13)

Long life and wellness

My son, do not forget my law, but let your heart guard my precepts. For they shall set before you length of days, and years of life, and peace. (Pro 3:1-2)

Whoever guards a commandment guards his own soul. But whoever neglects his own way will die. (Pro 19:16)

I will never forget your precepts: for by them you have kept me alive. (Ps 119:93)

Our Prayers will be answered

Whatever we shall request of him, we shall receive from him. For we keep his commandments, and we do the things that are pleasing in his sight. (1 Jn 3:22)

Who will grant to them to have such a mind, so that they may fear me, and may keep all my commandments at all times, so that it may be well with them and with their children forever? (Deut 5:29)

He said to him: "I am the Almighty God. Walk in my sight and become complete. And I will set my covenant between me and you. And I will multiply you very exceedingly." (Gen 17:1-2)

The Holy Spirit will rest on us

We are witnesses of these things, with the Holy Spirit, whom God has given to all who are obedient to him. (Acts 5:32)

Eternal life

If you wish to enter into life, observe the commandments. (Matt 19:17)

My child, guard my words and conceal my precepts within you. Preserve my commandments, and you shall live. And keep my law as the pupil of your eye. (Pro 7:1-2)

Financial blessings

If only you had paid attention to my commandments! Your prosperity would have been like a river, and your success would have been like the waves of the sea, and your offspring would have been like the sand, and the stock from your loins would have been like its stones. (Is 48:18-19)

Then you will be able to prosper, if you keep the commandments and judgments that the Lord instructed Moses to teach to Israel. (1 Chron 22:13)

Blessed are the immaculate in the way, who walk in the law of the Lord. Blessed are those who keep his decrees, who seek him with their whole heart. (Ps 119:1-2)

Healing

If you will listen to the voice of the Lord your God, and do what is right in his sight, and obey his commands, and keep all his precepts, I will not bring upon you any of the distress that I imposed on Egypt. For I am the Lord, your healer. (Exo 15:26)

Deliverance

For if you keep the commandments which I am entrusting to you, and if you do them, so that you love the Lord your God, and walk in all his ways, clinging to him, the Lord will drive out all these nations before your face, and you shall possess them, though they are greater and stronger than you. (Deut 11:22-23)

Spiritual gifts

If you desire wisdom, keep the commandments, and then God will offer her to you. (Wis 1:26)

Victory and Success

Therefore, keep the words of this covenant, and fulfill them, so that you may succeed in all that you are doing. (Deut 29:9)

We will be filled with God's love

As the Father has loved me, so I have loved you. Abide in my love. If you keep my commandments, you shall abide in my love, just as I also have kept my Father's commandments and I abide in his love. (Jn 15:9-10)

Protection from sin

For the commandment is a lamp, and law is a light, and the reproofs of discipline are the way of life. So may they guard you from an evil woman, and from the flattering tongue of the outsider. (Pro 6:23-24)

Complaining and grumbling

Brothers, do not complain against one another, so that you may not be judged. Behold, the judge stands before the door. (Jas 5:9)

Complex (inferiority)

The Lord will appoint you as the head, and not as the tail. And you shall be always above, and not beneath. But only if you will listen to the commandments of the Lord your God, which I entrust to you this day, and will keep and do them. (Deut 28:13)

Complex (Superiority)

Let nothing be done by contention, nor in vain glory. Instead, in humility, let each of you esteem others to be better than himself. (Phil 2:3)

Condemnation

God's promise for those who are facing condemnation
Therefore, there is now no condemnation for those who are in Christ Jesus. (Rom 8:1)

Confession

Prayer after confession
Create a clean heart in me, O God. And renew a right spirit within me. Do not cast me away from your presence; and do not take your Holy Spirit from me. Restore to me the joy of your salvation, and sustain in me with a willing spirit. (Ps 51:11-13)

Prayer of healing of the soul after confession
Lord, be merciful unto me: heal my soul; for I have sinned against you. (Ps 41:4)

What are the blessings we receive when we confess our sins?

Our sins are forgiven
If we confess our sins, then he who is faithful and just will forgive us our sins and cleanse us from all iniquity. (1 Jn 1:9)

I will cleanse them from all their iniquity, by which they have sinned against me. And I will forgive all their iniquities, by which they have offended against me and have despised me. (Jer 33:8)

We receive God's mercy
The Lord your God is compassionate and merciful, and he will not turn away his face from you, if you will return to him. (2 Chron 30:9)

He that hides his sins, shall not prosper: but he that shall confess, and forsake them, shall obtain mercy. (Pro 28:13)

We are freed of guilt
I said, "I will confess against myself, my injustice to the Lord," and you forgave the guilt of my sin. (Ps 32:5)

We are filled with Godly peace
Because I was silent, my bones grew old, while still I cried out all day long. For, day and night, your hand was heavy upon me. I have been converted in my anguish, while still the thorn is piercing. I have acknowledged my offense to you, and I have not concealed my injustice. I said, "I will confess against myself, my injustice to the Lord," and you forgave the guilt of my sin. (Ps 32:3-5)

We are healed (body, mind, soul, and spirit)
Confess your sins to one another, and pray for one another, so that you may be healed. The prayer of the righteous is powerful and effective. (Jas 5:16)

Do not seem wise to yourself. Fear God, and withdraw from evil. Certainly, it shall be health to your flesh, and refreshment to your body. (Pro 3:7-8)

God intervenes and helps us in life's struggles
Be sanctified. For tomorrow the Lord will accomplish miracles among you. (Josh 3:5)

We will be freed from addictions and sinful habits
He will turn back and have mercy on us. He will put away our iniquities, and he will cast all our sins into the depths of the sea. (Mic 7:19)

Our sins will be completely erased and forgotten by God
I will forgive their iniquity, and I will no longer remember their sin. (Jer 31:34)

I am. I am the very One who wipes away your iniquities for my own sake. And I will not remember your sins. (Is 43:25)

We will find peace with God and man
The son said to him: 'Father, I have sinned against heaven and before you. Now I am not worthy to be called your son.' But the father said to his servants: 'Quickly! Bring out the best robe, and clothe him with it. And put a ring on his hand and shoes on his feet. And bring the fatted calf here, and kill it. And let us eat and hold a feast. For this son of mine was dead, and has revived; he was lost, and is found.' And they began to feast. (Luk 15:21-24)

We are reconciled with God (Relationship is restored)
For if we were reconciled to God through the death of his Son, while we were still enemies, all the more so, having been reconciled, shall we be saved by his life. And not only that, but we also glory in God through our Lord Jesus Christ, through whom we have now received reconciliation. (Rom 5:10-11)

We are cleansed and renewed
I will pour clean water over you, and you shall be cleansed from all your filth, and I will cleanse you from all your idols. And I will give to you a new heart, and I will place in you a new spirit. And I will take away the heart of stone from your body, and I will give to you a heart of flesh. (Eze 36:25-26)

We are made holy
I am the Lord your God: you shall therefore sanctify yourselves, and you shall be holy; for I am holy. (Lev 11:44)

We are filled with God's presence
Go to the people, and sanctify them today, and tomorrow, and let them wash their garments. And let them be prepared on the third

day. For on the third day, the Lord will descend, in the sight of all the people, over Mount Sinai. (Exo 19:10-11)

Confession makes us worthy to receive the body and blood of Jesus
Whoever eats this bread, or drinks from the cup of the Lord, unworthily, shall be liable of the body and blood of the Lord. But let a man examine himself, and, in this way, let him eat from that bread, and drink from that cup. For whoever eats and drinks unworthily, eats and drinks a sentence against himself, not discerning it to be the body of the Lord. As a result, many are weak and sick among you, and many have fallen asleep. (1 Cor 11:27-30)

Contentment

God's Word for living in contentment
Keep your lives free from the love of money; be content with what you have. For he himself has said, "I will not leave you, and I will not abandon you." (Heb 13:5)

There is great gain in Godliness with contentment. For we brought nothing into this world, and there is no doubt that we can take nothing away. But, if we have food and some kind of covering, we will be content with these. (1 Tim 6:6-8)

I have learned to be content in whatever state I am. I know how to have little, and I know how to abound. I am prepared for anything, anywhere: either to be full or to be hungry, either to have abundance or to endure scarcity. (Phil 4:11-12)

Prayer of contentment
Two things I have asked of you; do not deny them to me before I die. Remove, far from me, vanity and lying words. Give me neither begging, nor wealth. Apportion to me only the necessities of my life, lest perhaps, being filled, I might be enticed into denial, and say:

'Who is the Lord?' Or, being compelled by destitution, I might steal, and then perjure myself in the name of my God. (Pro 30:7-9)

Country

God's promise for a nation that honors God
Blessed is the nation whose God is the Lord, the people whom he has chosen as his inheritance. (Ps 33:12)

Behold, you will call to a nation that you did not know. And nations that did not know you will rush to you, because of the Lord your God, the Holy One of Israel. For he has glorified you. (Is 55:5)

God's promise for a country that is ruled or attacked by another country
When the day comes, says the Lord of hosts: I will crush the yoke from their neck, and I will break open their chains. And foreigners will no longer rule over them. Instead, they will serve the Lord their God. (Jer 30:8-9)

I will protect this city, so that I may save it for my own sake. (Is 37:35)

Prayer for freedom from a wicked ruler (dictators)
O Lord our God, save us from his hand, so that all the kingdoms of the earth may know that you alone are the Lord God. (2 Kgs 19:19)

And now, O Lord our God, save us from his hand. And let all the kingdoms of the earth acknowledge that you alone are Lord. (Is 37:20)

Prayer for freedom if your country is ruled by another country
Save us, O God our savior! And gather us together, and rescue us from the nations, so that we may give thanks to your holy name, and may glory in your praise. (1 Chron 16:35)

Prayer for God's mercy if your country (people) is living in sin
O Lord of hosts, the God of Israel who sits upon the Cherubim: you alone are God of all the kingdoms of the earth. You have made heaven and earth. O Lord, incline your ear and listen. O Lord, open your eyes and see. (Is 37:16-17)

Courage

God's promise of courage
You, Lord, are my supporter, my glory, and the one who raises up my head. (Ps 3:3)

Credit card

God's warning to those who overuse credit cards
There is one who buys much for a small price, and who pays it back sevenfold. (Sir 20:12)

Cross (Power of the Cross)

God's promise of the power of the cross
The message about the Cross is certainly foolishness to those who are perishing. But to those who have been saved, that is, to us, it is the power of God. (1 Cor 1:18)

But far be it from me to boast, except in the cross of our Lord Jesus Christ, through which the world is crucified to me, and I to the world. (Gal 6:14)

He himself bore our sins in his body on the cross, so that we, having died to sin, would live for righteousness. By his wounds, you have been healed. (1 Pet 2:24)

Cursing

God's warning for those who curse

No man is able to rule over the tongue, a restless evil, full of deadly poison. By it we bless God the Father, and by it we speak evil of men, who have been made in the likeness of God. From the same mouth proceeds blessing and cursing. My brothers, these things ought not to be so! (Jas 3:8-10)

Bless those who are persecuting you: bless, and do not curse.(Rom 12:14)

D

Death

God's promise for those who have the fear of death
I am the Resurrection and the Life. Whoever believes in me, even though he has died, he shall live. And everyone who lives and believes in me will never die. (Jn 11:25-26)

Do not be afraid of those who kill the body, but are not able to kill the soul. But instead fear him who is able to destroy both soul and body in Hell. (Matt 10:28)

The souls of the just are in the hand of God and no torment of death will touch them. (Wis 3:1)

God's promise for those who are mourning the death of a loved one
Blessed are those who mourn, for they will be comforted. (Matt 5:4)

Prayer before death
Into your hands, I commend my spirit. You have redeemed me, O Lord, faithful God. (Ps 31:5)

Debt (financial debt)

God's promise for those who are in financial debt
When the Lord your God has blessed you, as he promised you, you shall lend money to many nations, and you yourselves shall borrow in return from no one. You shall rule over very many nations, and no one shall rule over you. (Deut 15:6)

The Lord will open his excellent treasury, the heavens, so that it may distribute rain in due time. And he will bless all the works of your hands. And you shall lend to many nations, but you yourself will borrow nothing from anyone. And the Lord will appoint you as the head, and not as the tail. And you shall be always above, and not beneath. (Deut 28:12-13)

Prayer for freedom from financial debt
From the depths, I have cried out to you, O Lord. O Lord, hear my voice. Let your ears be attentive to the voice of my supplication. (Ps 130:1-2)

Word of Joy to claim during financial crisis
Though the fig tree will not flower, and there will be no bud on the vines. Though the labor of the olive tree will be misleading, and the farmland will produce no food. Though the sheep will be cut off from the sheepfold, and there will be no herd at the manger. But I will rejoice in the Lord; and I will exult in the God of my salvation. (Hab 3:17-18)

Deliverance

God's promise of our authority over evil spirits
Behold, I have given you authority to tread upon snakes and scorpions, and upon all the powers of the enemy, and nothing will hurt you. (Luk 10:19)

Your hand will be exalted over your enemies, and all your adversaries will be cut off. (Mic 5:9)

Having called together his twelve disciples, he gave them authority over unclean spirits, to cast them out and to cure every sickness and every infirmity. (Matt 10:1)

God's promise of deliverance
When evening arrived, they brought to him many who had demons, and he cast out the spirits with a word. (Matt 8:16)

Behold, they brought him a man who was mute, having a demon. And after the demon was cast out, the mute man spoke. And the crowds wondered, saying, "Never has anything like this been seen in Israel." (Matt 9:32-33)

They were all so amazed that they inquired among themselves, saying: "What is this? And what is this new teaching? For with authority he commands even the unclean spirits, and they obey him." (Mrk 1:27)

Fear fell over them all. And they discussed this among themselves, saying: "What is this word? For with authority and power he commands the unclean spirits, and they depart." (Luk 4:36)

Demons departed from many of them, crying out and saying, "You are the son of God." And rebuking them, he would not permit them to speak. For they knew him to be the Christ. (Luk 4:41)

Jesus of Nazareth, whom God anointed with the Holy Spirit and with power, traveled around doing good and healing all those oppressed by the devil. For God was with him. (Acts 10:38)

They cried out to the Lord in their tribulation, and he freed them from their distress. And he led them out of darkness and the shadow of death, and he broke apart their chains. (Ps 107:13-14)

For if he is a true child of God, he will help him and deliver him from the hands of his adversaries. (Wis 2:18)

He has rescued us from the power of darkness, and he has transferred us into the kingdom of his beloved Son. (Col 1:13)

He delivered me, because he delighted in me. (Ps 18:19)

I will pursue my enemies, and crush them. And I will not turn back, until I consume them. I will consume them and break them apart, so that they cannot rise up; they will fall under my feet. (2 Sam 22:38-39)

His burden will be taken away from your shoulder, and his yoke will be taken away from your neck. (Is 10:27)

Prayer of Deliverance
Let my supplication come before you; deliver me according to your word. (Ps 119:170)

Demons (See Evil Spirits)

Depression

Prayer for healing of depression (sorrow)
O Lord, be merciful to me, for I have cried out to you all day long. Give joy to the soul of your servant, for I have lifted up my soul to you, Lord. (Ps 86:3-4)

How long, O Lord? Will you forget me until the end? How long will you turn your face away from me? How long must I bear pain in my soul, and have sorrow in my heart throughout the day? (Ps 13:1-2)

God's promise for those suffering with depression
Take off, O Jerusalem, the garment of your sorrow and affliction, and put on your beauty and the honor of that eternal glory, which you have from God. God will surround you with a double garment of righteousness, and he will set a crown on your head of everlasting honor. (Bar 5:1-2)

I will turn their mourning into gladness, and I will console them and gladden them after their sorrow. (Jer 31:13)

Amen, amen, I say to you, that you shall mourn and weep, but the world will rejoice. And you shall be greatly saddened, yet your sorrow shall be turned into joy. (Jn 16:20)

Desires (evil, sinful, worldly, fleshly desires)

God's warning for those who pursue evil desires

You should not pursue, in your strength, the desires of your heart. (Sir 5:2)

You should not go after your desires; instead, turn away from your own will. (Sir 18:30)

The grace of God our Savior has appeared to all men, instructing us to reject impiety and worldly desires, so that we may live soberly and justly and piously in this age. (Tit 2:12)

Each one is tempted by his own desires, having been enticed and drawn away. Thereafter, when desire has conceived, it gives birth to sin. (Jas 1:14-15)

Desires (Good and godly desires)

God's promise for our desires

Delight in the Lord, and he will grant to you the desires of your heart. (Ps 37:4)

Bless the Lord, O my soul, and do not forget all his recompenses. He forgives all your iniquities. He heals all your infirmities. He redeems your life from destruction. He crowns you with mercy and compassion. He satisfies your desire with good things. (Ps 103:2-5)

Despair (hopelessness)

God's Word for those who are in despair

Because you are precious and honorable in my eyes, I have loved you, and I will present men on behalf of you, and nations on behalf of your life. (Is 43:4)

We are afflicted in every way, but not crushed; perplexed, but not driven to despair; persecuted, but not forsaken; struck down, but not destroyed; always carrying in the body the death of Jesus, so that the life of Jesus may also be made visible in our bodies. (2 Cor 4:8-10, NRSVCE)

Desperation

God's Word for those who are desperate

My soul waits in silence for God alone? For from him is my salvation. Yes, he alone is my rock and my salvation. He is my fortress; I will never be moved. Yet, truly, My soul waits for God alone. For from him is my hope. For he is my rock and my Savior. He is my fortress; I will not be moved. In God is my salvation and my glory. He is the God of my help, and my hope is in God. (Ps 62:1-2,5-7)

Direction (Decision making)

I will instruct you and teach you in the way which you shall go: I will guide you with my eye upon you. (Ps 32:8)

Your ears will listen to the word of one admonishing you behind your back: "This is the way! Walk in it! And do not turn aside, neither to the right, nor to the left." (Is 30:21)

Thus says the Lord, your Redeemer, the Holy One of Israel: I am the Lord, your God, who teaches you for your own good, who guides you in the way that you should go. (Is 48:17)

Disability

God's promise for those who are disable (who need help with their daily activities)
Fear not. I will help you, says the Lord, your Redeemer, the Holy One of Israel. (Is 41:14)

I have lifted up my eyes to the mountains; from where will help come to me. My help is from the Lord, who made heaven and earth. (Ps 121:1-2)

I am the Lord your God. I hold you by your right hand, and I say to you: Do not be afraid. I will help you. (Is 41:13)

Discipline of God

What are the blessings we receive when we submit to God's discipline?
We will be blessed
Blessed is the man whom God corrects; therefore, do not reject the chastisement of the Lord. (Job 5:17)

God pours his love on those who submit to his discipline
Those whom I love, I rebuke and chastise. Therefore, be zealous and do penance. (Rev 3:19)

My son, do not be willing to neglect the discipline of the Lord. Neither should you become weary, while being rebuked by him. For whomever the Lord loves, he chastises. And every son whom he accepts, he scourges. (Heb 12:5-6)

We grow in holiness when we submit to God's discipline
Human parents, according to what seemed best to them, disciplined us for a short time: but he, for our good, that we might share his holiness. (Heb 12:10)

God disciplines us to bring us out of sin
For you have chastised man for iniquity. consuming like a moth what is dear to them. (Ps 39:11)

Discipline builds character in us
A correction benefits more with a wise man, than a hundred stripes with a fool. (Pro 17:10)

We will be able to understand God's word and we will be able to hear God's voice clearly
Give heed by my correction; I will pour out my spirit to you, and I will reveal my words to you. (Pro 1:23)

Discipline is rewarding
Now every discipline, in the present time, does not seem a gladness, of course, but a grief. But afterwards, it will repay a most peaceful fruit of righteousness to those who become trained in it. (Heb 12:11)

And though, in the sight of men, they suffered torments, their hope is full of immortality. Having been disciplined a little, they will be well compensated, because God has tested them and found them worthy of himself. (Wis 3:4-5)

God's discipline leads us to eternal life
When we are judged, we are being corrected by the Lord, so that we might not be condemned along with this world. (1 Cor 11:32)

A person disciplined by God will flee from evil
Wisdom will not enter a deceitful soul, or dwell in a body enslaved to sin. For a holy and disciplined spirit will flee from deceit, and will

leave foolish thoughts behind, and will be ashamed at the approach of unrighteousness. (Wis 1:4-5)

God disciplines us to bring us to repentance
O how good and gracious, Lord, is your spirit in all things! Therefore, those who wander afield, you correct, and, as to those who sin, you counsel them and admonish them, so that, having abandoned malice, they may believe in you, O Lord. (Wis 12:1-2)

Accepting God's discipline will bring spiritual gifts (Holy Spirit) in us
Give heed by my correction; I will pour out my spirit to you, and I will reveal my words to you. (Pro 1:23)

Prayer to seek God's Discipline
Correct me, O Lord, yet truly, do so with judgment, and not in your fury. Otherwise, you will reduce me to nothing. (Jer 10:23)

Discouragement

Be strong and courageous; be not afraid, neither be dismayed: for the Lord your God is with you wherever you go. (Josh 1:9)

Be vigilant. Stand firm in faith. Be courageous and be strengthened. (1 Cor 16:13)

Distraction
Verse to meditate for those who are distracted
You will keep him in perfect peace, whose mind is stayed on you: because he trusts in you. (Is 26:2)

Distress

This is my comfort in my distress: for your promises gives me life. (Ps 119:50)

They cried out to the Lord in their tribulation, and he freed them from their distress. (Ps 107:13)

I will exult in Jerusalem, and I will rejoice in my people. And neither a voice of weeping, nor a cry of distress, will be heard in her anymore. (Is 65:19)

Divine Mercy Chaplet

What are the blessings we receive by seeking God's mercy?

Sicknesses are healed

Going out, he saw a great multitude, and he took pity on them, and he cured their sick. (Matt 14:14)

They said to him, "Lord, that our eyes be opened." Then Jesus, moved with compassion, touched their eyes. And immediately they saw, and they followed him. (Matt 20:33-34)

Pleading for God's mercy draws his attention to our needs

Bartimaeus, the son of Timaeus, a blind man, sat begging beside the way. And when he had heard that it was Jesus of Nazareth, he began to cry out and to say, "Jesus, Son of David, have mercy on me." And many admonished him to be quiet. But he cried out all the more, "Son of David, take pity on me." And Jesus, standing still, instructed him to be called. (Matt 10:46-48)

Prayer to seek God's mercy

Gaze down from heaven, and behold from your holy habitation and from your glory. Where is your zeal, and your strength, the fullness of your heart and of your compassion? They have held themselves back from me. (Is 63:15)

Divorce and Separation

God's advice and warning to all seeking divorce

From the beginning of creation, God made them male and female. Because of this, a man shall leave behind his father and mother, and he shall cling to his wife. And these two shall be one in flesh. And so, they are now, not two, but one flesh. Therefore, what God has joined together, let no man separate. (Mrk 10:6-9)

Whoever divorces his wife, and marries another, commits adultery against her. And if a wife divorces her husband, and is married to another, she commits adultery. (Mrk 10:11-12)

Are you bound to a wife? Do not seek to be freed. (1 Cor 7:27)

To those who have been joined in matrimony, it is not I who commands you, but the Lord: a wife is not to separate from her husband. (1 Cor 7:10)

Take heed to your spirit, and let none deal treacherously against the wife of his youth. For the Lord, the God of Israel, says that he hates divorce. (Mal 2:15-16)

Doctor

What does the Bible say about Doctors?

Honor the physician because of their services, because the Most High created him. For his gift of healing is from God, and so he is rewarded by the King. The expertise of the physician makes them unique, and in the sight of great men, he will be praised. (Sir 38:1-3)

Doubt and confusion

Word to meditate for those who are filled with doubt about God

He who doubts is like a wave on the ocean, which is moved about by the wind and carried away; then a man should not consider that he would receive anything from the Lord. For a man who is double-minded is unstable in all his ways. (Jas 1:6-8)

Amen I say to you, that whoever will say to this mountain, 'Be taken up and cast into the sea,' and who will not have doubted in his heart, but will have believed: then whatever he has said be done, it shall be done for him. (Mrk 11:23)

Amen I say to you, if you have faith and do not doubt, not only shall you do this, concerning the fig tree, but even if you would say to this mountain, 'Take and cast yourself into the sea,' it shall be done. (Matt 21:21)

Driving

God's promise for those who have fear of driving

I am the Lord your God. I hold you by your right hand, and I say to you: Do not be afraid. I will help you. (Is 41:13)

Your justifier shall go before you, the glory of the Lord shall be your rear guard. (Is 58:8-9)

Drug Addiction

God's warning for Drug Addicts

Do not court death by the error of your life, nor procure your destruction by the works of your hands. (Wis 1:12)

For if, after taking refuge from the defilements of the world in the understanding of our Lord and Savior Jesus Christ, they again become entangled and overcome by these things, then the latter state becomes worse than the former. (2 Pet 2:20)

Behold, all you who kindle a fire, wrapped in flames: walk in the light of your fire and in the flames that you have kindled. This is what you shall have from my hand; You will sleep in anguish. (Is 50:11)

Promise for parents of children who are addicted to drugs
Even the captives will be taken away from the strong, even what has been taken by the powerful will be saved. And truly, I will contend with those who contend with you, and I will save your children. (Is 49:25)

E

Education (Students)

God's promise for students who have difficulty studying and understanding concepts
The Lord bestows wisdom, and out of his mouth, understanding and knowledge. (Pro 2:6)

All your children will be taught by the Lord. And great will be the prosperity of your children. (Is 54:13)

Blessing of parents for children who are leaving home for college or job
The Lord will guard you from all evil. He will guard your life. The Lord will guard your entrance and your exit, from this time and forevermore. (Ps 121:7-8)

Prayer of students who need help with public speaking
Alas, Lord God! Behold, I do not know how to speak, for I am a boy (girl). (Jer 1:7)

Employers

Prayer over employees
O Lord, bless his substance, and receive the works of his hands. (Deut 33:11)

God's advice for employers
Whoever has done any kind of work for you, immediately pay him his wages, and do not let the wages of your hired hand remain with you at all. (Tob 4:14)

You should not harm the servant whose works are honest, nor the hired hand who entrusts his life to you. Let an understanding servant be loved by you like your own soul. You should not cheat him out of freedom, nor abandon him to destitution. (Sir 7:20-21)

Enemies

God's promise for those who are troubled by enemies
What should we say about these things? If God is for us, who is against us? (Rom 8:31)

For if he is a true child of God, he will help him and deliver him from the hands of his adversaries. (Wis 2:18)

I will call upon the Lord, who is worthy to be praised: so shall I be saved from my enemies. (Ps 18:3)

I will present you to this people as a strong wall of brass. And they will fight against you, and they will not prevail. For I am with you, so as to save you and to rescue you, says the Lord. (Jer 15:20)

When the ways of man will please the Lord, even his enemies will be at peace with him. (Pro 16:7)

God's Word about our attitude toward our enemies
If your enemy is hungry, feed him. If he is thirsty, give him water to drink. For you will gather hot coals upon his head, and the Lord will repay you. (Pro 25:21-22)

But I say to you: Love your enemies. Do good to those who hate you. And pray for those who persecute and slander you. (Matt 5:44)

God's promise for us when people device evil against us
All who fight against you shall be confounded and ashamed. They will be as if they did not exist, and the men who contradict you will perish. You will seek them, and you will not find them. The men who rebel against you will be as if they did not exist. And the men who

make war against you will be like something that has been consumed. For I, the Lord your God, hold your right hand; it is I who say to you, "Do not fear, I will help you." (Is 41:11-13)

They will make war against you, but they will not prevail. For I am with you, says the Lord, so that I may deliver you. (Jer 1:19)

Envy

God's advice and warning against envy
When your enemy will fall, do not be glad, and do not let your heart exult in his ruin. (Pro 24:17)

Whoever enjoys the fall of the just will perish in a snare, and grief will consume them before they die. (Sir 27:29)

Let us not become desirous of empty glory, competing against one another, envying one another. (Gal 5:26)

Do not envy evil men, nor desire to be among them. For their mind meditates on robberies, and their lips speak deceptions. (Pro 24:1-2)

Eternal Life

How to attain eternal life?
Believe in Jesus (Accept Jesus as the lord of your life through Baptism)
God so loved the world that he gave his only-begotten Son, so that all who believe in him may not perish, but may have eternal life. (Jn 3:16)

Do the will of God in all things
The world is passing away, with its desire. But whoever does the will of God abides unto eternity. (1 Jn 2:17)

Obey the commandments
If you wish to enter into life, observe the commandments. (Matt 19:17)

Receive Jesus in the Eucharist (sacramental life)
I am the living bread, who descended from heaven. If anyone eats from this bread, he shall live forever. (Jn 6:51)

Eucharist (Holy Mass)

Prayer before receiving communion
Lord, I am not worthy that you should enter under my roof, but only say the word, and my servant shall be healed. (Matt 8:8)

God's warning for those who receive communion in a state of mortal sin
Whoever eats this bread, or drinks from the cup of the Lord, unworthily, shall be liable of the body and blood of the Lord. (1 Cor 11:27)

Whoever eats and drinks unworthily, eats and drinks a sentence against himself, not discerning it to be the body of the Lord. As a result, many are weak and sick among you, and many have fallen asleep. (1 Cor 11:29-30)

What are the blessings of receiving Jesus in the Eucharist?

The Eucharist unites us with other believers
Through the one bread, we, though many, are one body: all of us who are partakers of the one bread. (1 Cor 10:17)

The Eucharist gives us revelation, knowledge, and understanding of Jesus

It happened that, while he was at table with them, he took bread, and he blessed and broke it, and he extended it to them. And their eyes were opened, and they recognized him.. (Luk 24:30-31)

They explained the things that were done on the way, and how they had recognized him at the breaking of the bread. (Luk 24:35)

The Eucharist is our food (it nourishes and strengthens us)

No man has ever hated his own flesh, but instead he nourishes and cherishes it, as Christ also does to the Church. For we are a part of his body, of his flesh and of his bones. (Eph 5:29-30)

Do not work for food that perishes, but for that which endures to eternal life, which the Son of man will give to you. (Jn 6:27)

Jesus said to them: "I am the bread of life. Whoever comes to me shall not hunger, and whoever believes in me shall never thirst." (Jn 6:35)

The Eucharist unites God with Man

But now, in Christ Jesus, you, who were in times past far away, have been brought near by the blood of Christ. For he is our peace. He made the two into one, by dissolving the intermediate wall of separation, of opposition, by his flesh, emptying the law of commandments by decree, so that he might join these two, in himself, into one new man, making peace and reconciling both to God, in one body, through the cross, destroying this opposition in himself. (Eph 2:13-16)

The Eucharist brings us into the presence of God

Whoever eats my flesh and drinks my blood abides in me, and I in him. (Jn 6:57)

The Eucharist keeps us away from sin

Everyone who abides in him does not sin. For whoever sins has not seen him, and has not known him. (1 Jn 3:6)

The Eucharist helps us overcome our flesh (sinful) nature

Let us walk honestly, as in the daylight, not in carousing and drunkenness, not in promiscuity and sexual immorality, not in contention and envy. Instead, be clothed with the Lord Jesus Christ, and make no provision for the flesh in its desires. (Rom 13:13-14)

The Eucharist gives us eternal life

I am the living bread, who descended from heaven. If anyone eats from this bread, he shall live forever. (Jn 6:51)

This is the bread which descends from heaven, so that if anyone will eat from it, he may not die. (Jn 6:50)

Whoever eats my flesh and drinks my blood has eternal life, and I will raise him up on the last day. (Jn 6:54)

This is the bread that descends from heaven. It is not like the manna that your fathers ate, for they died. Whoever eats this bread shall live forever. (Jn 6:58)

The Eucharist gives us inner life (love, joy, and peace in our heart)

Jesus said to them: "Amen, amen, I say to you, unless you eat the flesh of the Son of man and drink his blood, you will not have life in you." (Jn 6:53)

Just as the living Father has sent me and I live because of the Father, so also whoever eats me will live because of me. (Jn 6:57)

The Eucharist gives us life around us (life in the world)

The bread that I will give is my flesh, for the life of the world. (Jn 6:51)

Amen, amen, I say to you, Moses did not give you bread from heaven, but my Father gives you the true bread from heaven. For the bread of God is he who descends from heaven and gives life to the world. (Jn 6:32-33)

Amen, amen, I say to you, unless you eat the flesh of the Son of man and drink his blood, you will not have life in you. (Jn 6:53)

The Eucharist enables us to bear good fruits
Abide in me as I abide in you. Just as the branch is not able to bear fruit of itself, unless it abides in the vine, so also are you unable, unless you abide in me. (Jn 15:4)

I am the vine; you are the branches. Whoever abides in me, and I in him, bears much fruit. For without me, you can do nothing. (Jn 15:5)

Eucharistic Adoration

What are the blessings of adoring Jesus in the Blessed Sacrament?
We find rest in the presence of God
Come to me, all you who labor and have been burdened, and I will give you rest. (Matt 11:28)

Jesus in the tabernacle fills our inner hunger and thirst
I am the bread of life. Whoever comes to me shall not hunger, and whoever believes in me shall never thirst. (Jn 6:35)

Jesus speaks to us
She had a sister, named Mary, who, while sitting beside the Lord's feet, was listening to his word. (Luk 10:39)

We grow in love for Jesus
When he returned to the camp, his minister Joshua, the son of Nun, a young man, did not withdraw from the Tabernacle. (Exo 33:11)

He said to Peter: "So, were you not able to keep vigil with me for one hour? (Ps 26:40)

She was a widow, even to her eighty-fourth year. And without departing from the temple, she was a servant to fasting and prayer, night and day. (Luk 2:37)

We are filled with God's love
Through the abundance of your steadfast love, I will enter your house. I will show adoration toward your holy temple, in your fear. (Ps 5:7)

We are filled with God's presence
Jesus, being tired from the journey, was sitting in a certain way on the well. It was about the sixth hour. A woman of Samaria arrived to draw water. Jesus said to her, "Give me to drink." (Jn 4:6-7)

I will set my tabernacle in your midst, and my soul will not cast you out. I will walk among you, and I will be your God, and you shall be my people. (Lev 26:11-12)

We receive insights into spiritual matters
I considered, so that I might know this. It is a hardship before me, until I may enter into the Sanctuary of God, and understand it to its end. (Ps 73:16-17)

Our family will be blessed
The ark of God dwelt in the house of Obededom for three months. And the Lord blessed his house and all that he had. (1 Chron 13:14)

Evangelization

God's word for those who are afraid and shy of evangelizing
I am not ashamed of the Gospel. For it is the power of God unto salvation for all believers, the Jew first, and the Greek. (Rom 1:16)

God's promise when we evangelize

He said to them: "Go forth to the whole world and preach the Gospel to every creature. Whoever will have believed and been baptized will be saved. Yet truly, whoever will not have believed will be condemned. (Mrk 16:15-16)

How beautiful upon the mountains are the feet of the messenger who announces peace! Who brings good news, who announces salvation. They are saying to Zion, "Your God will reign!" (Is 52:7)

Prayer to ask God for evangelizers

I beg you Lord, that the man of God, whom you sent, may come again, and may teach us what we ought to do. (Jdgs 13:8)

Prayer of evangelists

Here I am. Send me. (Is 6:8)

What are the blessings we receive when we evangelize?

We will be saved

For if you confess with your mouth the Lord Jesus, and if you believe in your heart that God has raised him up from the dead, you shall be saved. For with the heart, we believe and we are justified; and with the mouth, we confess and we are saved. (Rom 10:9-10)

Jesus will intercede for us

Everyone who acknowledges me before men, I also will acknowledge before my Father, who is in heaven. But whoever will have denied me before men, I also will deny before my Father, who is in heaven. (Matt 10:32-33)

God will be with us

Those who fear the Lord spoke, each one with his neighbor. And the Lord paid attention and heeded. And a book of remembrance was written in his sight, for those who fear the Lord and for those who consider his name. And they will be my special possession, says the Lord of hosts, on the day that I act. (Mal 3:16-17)

Our faith will increase when we evangelize
Go to your own people, in your own house, and announce to them how great are the things that the Lord has done for you, and how he has taken pity on you. (Mrk 5:19)

God will perform signs and wonders when we evangelize
They went forth, and preached the good news everywhere, the Lord worked with them, and confirmed the word with signs that accompanied it. (Mrk 16:20)

Evil Spirits (Demons)

God's promise of our authority over evil spirits and demons
He acted so that the twelve would be with him, and so that he might send them out to preach. And he gave them authority to cure infirmities, and to cast out demons. (Mrk 3:14-15)

He called the twelve. And he began to send them out in twos, and he gave them authority over unclean spirits. (Mrk 6:7)

Behold, I have given you authority to tread upon serpents and scorpions, and upon all the powers of the enemy, and nothing shall hurt you. (Luk 10:19)

The Lord will grant that your enemies, who rise up against you, will be defeated in your sight. They will come against you by one way, and they will flee from your face by seven ways. (Deut 28:7)

Then calling together the twelve Apostles, Jesus gave them power and authority over all demons and to cure diseases. (Luk 9:1)

You will trample the wicked, while they will be ashes under the sole of your foot, on the day that I act, says the Lord of hosts. (Mal 4:3)

Examination of Conscience

God's promise for those who examine their conscience
You also are saved, in a similar manner, by baptism, not by the testimony of sordid flesh, but by the examination of a good conscience in God, through the resurrection of Jesus Christ. (1 Pet 3:21)

Eye

Bible verses to meditate for those who have lustful, worldly, greedy, and covetous eyes
The lamp of your body is your eye. If your eye is wholesome, your entire body will be filled with light. But if your eye has been corrupted, your entire body will be darkened. If then the light that is in you is darkness, how great will that darkness be! (Matt 6:22-23)

I will not display any unjust thing before my eyes. (Ps 101:3)

Let your eyes look straight ahead, and let your eyelids precede your steps. Direct the path of your feet, and all your ways shall be secure. Turn aside, neither to the right, nor to the left; yet turn your foot away from evil. For the Lord knows the ways that are on the right, and truly, those that are on the left are perverse. (Pro 4:25-26)

You have heard that it was said to the ancients: 'You shall not commit adultery.' But I say to you, that anyone who will have looked at a woman, so as to lust after her, has already committed adultery with her in his heart. And if your right eye causes you to sin, root it out and cast it away from you. For it is better for you that one of your members perish, than that your whole body be cast into Hell. (Matt 5:27-29)

You should not stare at a virgin, lest perhaps you may be scandalized by her beauty. (Sir 9:5)

Avert your eyes from a shapely woman, for you should not gaze upon beauty belonging to another. (Sir 9:8)

I reached an agreement with my eyes, how then could I gaze at a virgin. (Job 31:1)

Let each one cast away the offenses of his eyes, and do not choose to defile yourselves with the idols of Egypt. I am the Lord your God. (Eze 20:7)

Prayer for the purification of our eyes
Lord, Father and God of my life. Do not leave me with the haughtiness of my eyes.(Sir 23:5)

Turn my eyes away, lest they see what is vain. Revive me in your way. (Ps 119:37)

F

Failure

Word to meditate when faced with defeat and failure
Do not be afraid, and do not dread or have fear of them. For the Lord your God himself goes with you, and he will neither fail you nor abandon you. (Deut 31:6)

Shake yourself from the dust! Arise and sit up, O Jerusalem! Loose the chains from your neck, O captive! (Is 52:2)

Arise, shine; for your light has come, O Jerusalem! For your light has arrived, and the glory of the Lord has risen over you. For behold, darkness will cover the earth, and thick darkness will cover the peoples. Then the Lord will rise above you, and his glory will be seen in you. And the nations will walk in your light, and the kings will walk by the splendor of your rising. (Is 60:1-3)

Faith

What are the blessings we receive for having faith?
Faith makes God intervene
And to the centurion Jesus said, "Go; let it be done for you according to your faith." And the servant was healed in that hour. (Matt 8:13)

All things whatever you ask for when praying, believe that you have received them, and they will be yours. (Mrk 11:24)

Faith helps us experience God
Without faith, it is impossible to please God. For whoever approaches God must believe that he exists, and that he rewards those who seek him. (Heb 11:6)

Faith answers prayers
All things whatsoever that you shall ask for in prayer with faith, you shall receive. (Matt 21:22)

Faith helps us to experience supernatural things
Amen I say to you, certainly, if you will have faith like a grain of mustard seed, you will say to this mountain, 'Move from here to there,' and it shall move. And nothing will be impossible for you. (Matt 17:19-20)

Amen I say to you, that whoever will say to this mountain, 'Be taken up and cast into the sea,' and who will not have doubted in his heart, but will have believed: then whatever he has said be done, it shall be done for him. (Mrk 11:23)

He did not work many miracles there, because of their unbelief. (Matt 13:58)

Amen I say to you, if you have faith and do not doubt, not only shall you do this, concerning the fig tree, but even if you would say to this mountain, 'Take and cast yourself into the sea,' it shall be done. (Matt 21:21)

Our faith can bring God's intervention in others' lives
They brought to him a paralytic, lying on a bed. And Jesus, seeing their faith, said to the paralytic, "Be strengthened in faith, son; your sins are forgiven you." (Matt 9:2)

Faith saves us
If you confess with your mouth the Lord Jesus, and if you believe in your heart that God has raised him up from the dead, you shall be saved. (Rom 10:9)

Our faith can save all those we love and pray for
Behold, some men were carrying in the bed of a man who was paralyzed. And they sought a way to bring him in, and to place him before him. And not finding a way by which they might bring him in, because of the crowd, they climbed up to the roof, and they let him down through the roof tiles with his bed, into their midst, in front of Jesus. And when he saw his faith, he said, "Man, your sins are forgiven you." (Luk 5:18-20)

Faith justifies us
The end of the law, Christ, is unto righteousness for all who believe. (Rom 10:4)

Faith fills us with peace
Therefore, having been justified by faith, we are at peace with God, through our Lord Jesus Christ. (Rom 5:1)

Faith will make us see impossible things
If you are able to believe: all things are possible to one who believes. (Mrk 9:23)

Faith can heal us
When he had arrived at the house, the blind men approached him. And Jesus said to them, "Do you trust that I am able to do this for you?" They say to him, "Certainly, Lord." Then he touched their eyes, saying, "According to your faith, so let it be done for you." And their eyes were opened. (Matt 9:28-30)

He said to her: "Daughter, your faith has saved you. Go in peace, and be healed from your wound." (Mrk 5:34)

God's promise for prayers made with faith
All things whatsoever that you ask for when praying: believe that you have received it, and it will be yours. (Mrk 11:24)

All things whatsoever that you shall ask for in prayer with faith, you shall receive. (Matt 21:22)

Amen I say to you, that whoever will say to this mountain, 'Be taken up and cast into the sea,' and who will not have doubted in his heart, but will have believed: then whatever he has said be done, it shall be done for him. (Mrk 11:23)

Prayer for faith
Lord, Increase our faith. (Luk 17:5)

Faithfulness

If we are unfaithful, he remains faithful: for he cannot deny himself. (2 Tim 2:13)

Endure steadfastly for God. Stay with God, and persevere, so that your life may be prosperous in the very end. (Sir 2:3)

False Accusation

God's promise for those who are falsely accused
He who justifies me is near. Who will speak against me? Let us stand together. Who is my adversary? Let him approach me. Behold, the Lord God is my helper. Who is the one who would condemn me? Behold, they will all be worn away like a garment; the moth will devour them. (Is 50:8-9)

Family

Prayer for the healing of the family tree and the forgiveness of sins of the ancestors

Do not remember against us the iniquities of our ancestors. May your mercies quickly meet us, for we have become exceedingly poor. (Ps 79:8)

O Lord, we acknowledge our impieties, the iniquities of our ancestors, that we have sinned against you. For the sake of your name, do not give us over into disgrace. And do not dishonor the throne of your glory. Remember, do not make void, your covenant with us. (Jer 14:20-21)

Family blessing prayer

Bless the house of your servant, so that it may be forever before you. For you, O Lord God, have spoken. And so, let the house of your servant be blessed with your blessing forever. (2 Sam 7:29)

Prayer to bless the family (Prayer of Jabez)

If only, when blessing, you will bless me, and will broaden my borders, and your hand will be with me, and you will keep me from hurt and harm. (1 Chron 4:10)

Blessing prayer over families for their finances

May the Lord increase you more and more, you and your children. May you be blessed by the Lord who made heaven and earth. (Ps 115:14-15)

Prayer for God's blessing upon our family

Now therefore, O Lord God, you are God, and your words shall be true. For you have spoken to your servant these good things. Therefore, begin, and bless the house of your servant, so that it may be forever before you. For you, O Lord God, have spoken. And so, let the house of your servant be blessed with your blessing forever. (2 Sam 7:28-29)

Psalm 128 (God's promise for families)

Blessed are all those who fear the Lord, who walk in his ways.

For you will eat the fruit of the labors of your hands. Blessed are you, and it will be well with you.

Your wife is like an abundant vine within your house. Your children are like young olive trees surrounding your table.

Behold, so will the man be blessed who fears the Lord.

May the Lord bless you from Zion, and may you see the good things of Jerusalem, all the days of your life.

And may you see the children of your children. Peace be upon Israel.

God's promise for families

Believe in the Lord Jesus, and then you will be saved, you and your household. (Acts 16:31)

The Lord has been mindful of us, and he has blessed us. He has blessed the house of Israel. He has blessed the house of Aaron. He has blessed all who fear the Lord, the small with the great. (Ps 115:12-13)

Happy is the man who fears the Lord, who will delight in his commandments exceedingly. His offspring will be powerful on the earth. The generation of the upright will be blessed. Glory and wealth will be in his house, and his justice shall remain from age to age. (Ps 112:1-3)

May our sons be like new plantings in their youth. Our daughters be dressed up: adorned all around like cornerstones of a temple. May our barns be full: overflowing from one thing into another. Our sheep bear young, brought forth in abundance. May our cattle be heavy with young. May there be no ruined wall or passage, nor anyone crying out in our streets. (Ps 144:12-14)

Enlarge the place of your tent and extend the curtains of your habitations, unsparingly. Lengthen your cords, and strengthen your stakes. For you shall extend to the right and to the left. And your offspring shall inherit the nations, and you shall inhabit the desolate cities. (Is 54:2-3)

Family prayer of commitment to God
As for me and my household, we will serve the Lord. (Josh 24:15)

Thanksgiving prayer for the gift of family
Who am I, O Lord God, and what is my house, that you would bring me to this point? (2 Sam 7:18)

Family Prayer

God's promise for those who pray as a family
Again I say to you, that if two of you have agreed on earth, about anything whatsoever that you have requested, it shall be done for you by my Father, who is in heaven. For wherever two or three are gathered in my name, there am I, in their midst. (Matt 18:19-20)

Farmer, Agriculture

Farmer's prayer of thanksgiving for harvest
I bring the first of the fruit of the ground that you, O Lord, have given me. (Deut 26:10)

God's promise to farmers
Those who sow in tears shall reap with shouts of joy. When departing, they went forth and wept, sowing their seeds. But when returning, they will arrive with shouts of joy, carrying their sheaves. (Ps 126:5-6)

Wherever you sow seed upon the earth, rain will be given to the seed. And bread from the grain of the earth will be very plentiful and full. In that day, the lamb will pasture in the spacious land of your possession. And your bulls, and the colts of the donkeys that work the ground, will eat a mix of grains like that winnowed on the threshing floor. (Is 30:23-24)

I will plant the cedar in a deserted place, with the thorn, and the myrtle, and the olive tree. In the desert, I will plant the pine, and the elm, and the box tree together, so that they may see and know, acknowledge and understand, together, that the hand of the Lord has accomplished this, and that the Holy One of Israel has created it. (Is 41:19-20)

Fasting

What are the blessings we receive when we fast?

Fasting is a sign of humility (we grow in humility)
All the people cried out to the Lord with great urgency, and they humbled their souls with fasting, and prayer, both they and their wives. (Judith 4:9)

I humbled my soul with fasting. (Ps 69:10)

When Ahab had heard these words, he tore his garments, and he put haircloth on his body, and he fasted, and he slept in sackcloth, and he walked with his head downcast. And the word of the Lord came to Elijah, the Tishbite, saying: "Have you not seen how Ahab has humbled himself before me? Therefore, since he has humbled himself because of me, I will not lead in the evil during his days. Instead, during the days of his son, I will bring in the evil to his house." (1 Kgs 21:27-29)

Fasting is a sign of repentance and penance (We grow in repentance)

The men of Nineveh believed in God. And they proclaimed a fast, and they put on sackcloth, from the greatest all the way to the least. (Jon 3:5)

On that day they fasted, and in that place they said, "We have sinned against the Lord." (1 Sam 7:6)

Fasting loosens the power of evil over us

Is not this, instead, the kind of fast that I have chosen? Release the constraints of impiety; relieve the burdens that oppress; freely forgive those who are broken; and break apart every burden. (Is 58:6)

This kind is not cast out, except through prayer and fasting. (Matt 17:21)

Fasting is an act of thanksgiving to God (We grow in thanksgiving)

He who observes the day, observes for the Lord. And he who eats, eats for the Lord; for he gives thanks to God. And he who does not eat, does not eat for the Lord, and he gives thanks to God. (Rom 14:6)

Fasting and prayer helps us to know the will of God

Now as they were ministering for the Lord and fasting, the Holy Spirit said to them: "Separate Saul and Barnabas for me, for the work for which I have selected them." Then, fasting and praying and imposing their hands upon them, they sent them away. (Acts 13:2-3)

Fasting and prayer increases our faith

When he had entered into the house, his disciples questioned him privately, "Why were we unable to cast him out?" And he said to them, "This kind is able to be expelled by nothing other than prayer and fasting." (Mrk 9:27-28)

Fasting and prayer helps us get God's help and intervention
Messengers arrived and reported to Jehoshaphat, saying: "A great multitude has arrived against you, from those places that are across the sea, and from Syria. And behold, they are standing together at Hazazon-tamar, which is Engedi." Then Jehoshaphat, being terrified with fear, gave himself entirely to petitioning the Lord, and he proclaimed a fast for all of Judah. And Judah gathered together to pray to the Lord. (2 Chron 20:2-3)

Fasting helps us grow in self denial
I proclaimed a fast in that place, beside the river Ahava, so that we might deny ourselves in the sight of the Lord our God, and so that we might request of him the right way for us, and for our sons, and for all our substance. (Ezra 8:21)

Fasting (with prayer) delivers us from demons and evil spirits
When he had entered into the house, his disciples questioned him privately, "Why were we unable to cast him out?" And he said to them, "This kind is able to be expelled by nothing other than prayer and fasting." (Mrk 9:27-28)

Fear

God's Promise for those in fear
Those who fear the Lord will tremble at nothing, and they will not be terrified. For he is their hope. (Sir 34:16)

God's promise of the Holy Spirit for those who are in fear
My Spirit is in your midst. Do not be afraid. (Hag 2:5)

God's promise for those who are in fear because of life's problems
He said, "Fear not, O man of longing. May peace be with you. Take courage and be strong." And when he spoke to me, I was strengthened, and I said, "Speak, my lord, for you have strengthened me." (Dan 10:19)

There is no fear in love. Instead, perfect love casts out fear, for fear pertains to punishment. And whoever fears is not perfected in love. (1 Jn 4:18)

Promises to claim for some common types of fears

Fear of darkness

Be strong and courageous; be not afraid, neither be dismayed: for the Lord your God is with you wherever you go. (Josh 1:9)

Even though I walk through the valley of the shadow of death, I will fear no evil: for you are with me; Your rod and your staff they comfort me. (Ps 23:4)

Fear of driving

I am the Lord your God. I hold you by your right hand, and I say to you: Do not be afraid. I will help you. (Is 41:13)

Fear of death

Do not be afraid of those who kill the body, but are not able to kill the soul. But instead fear him who is able to destroy both soul and body in Hell. (Matt 10:28)

Fear of incurable sicknesses

This sickness is not unto death, but for the glory of God, so that the Son of God may be glorified by it. (Jn 11:4)

Fear of exams, test, and interviews

Do not be afraid, and do not dread or have fear of them. For the Lord your God himself goes with you, and he will neither fail you nor abandon you. (Deut 31:6)

Fear of Satan, Ghosts, and evil spirits

Little children, you are of God, and so you have conquered him. For he who is in you is greater than he who is in the world. (1 Jn 4:4)

Strengthen the weak hands, and make firm the weak knees! Say to the fainthearted: "Take courage and fear not! Behold, your God will come with vengeance. God himself will come to save you." (Is 35:3-4)

Fear of sudden disaster (trauma)

Do not fear unexpected terror, nor the power of the impious falling upon you. For the Lord will be at your side, and he will guard your feet, so that you may not be seized. (Pro 3:25-26)

You will be established in righteousness. You shall be far from oppression, for you will not be afraid. And from terror, for it will not come near you. (Is 54:14)

Fear of people

In God, I have trusted. I will not fear what man can do to me. (Ps 56:11)

The Lord is my helper. I will not fear what man can do to me. (Heb 13:6)

It is I, I myself, who will comfort you. Why then would you be afraid of a mortal man who must die, a human who will wither like the grass? (Is 51:12)

Fear of failure and defeat

Do not be afraid, and do not dread or have fear of them. For the Lord your God himself goes with you, and he will neither fail you nor abandon you. (Deut 31:6)

Fear of economic downfall (Stock market collapse, etc.)

"You should not say 'It is conspiracy!' For all that this people speaks is a conspiracy. And you should not be frightened or alarmed with their fear. The Lord of hosts, him you shall regard holy. Let him be your dread, and let him be your fear. (Is 8:12-13)

Fear of losing job, losing savings
Behold, God is my savior, I will trust, and I will not be afraid. For the Lord is my strength and my might, and he has become my salvation. (Is 12:2)

Fear of persecution in ministry
Thus says the Lord, who made and formed you, and will help you: Do not be afraid, my servant and my most righteous, whom I have chosen. (Is 44:2)

Fear of insults, ridicule, and persecution by people
Do not be afraid of disgrace among men, and do not dread when they revile you. For the worm will consume them like a garment, and the moth will devour them like wool. But my deliverance will be forever, and my salvation will be from generation to generation. (Is 51:7-8)

As for you, mortal, you should not fear them, and you should not dread their words. For you are among unbelievers and subversives, and you are living with scorpions. You should not fear their words, and you should not dread their faces. (Eze 2:6)

Fear of God (Piety)

What are the blessings we receive for having fear of God in us?

Our families will be blessed
Happy is everyone who fears the Lord; who walks in his ways. For you shall eat the labor of your hands: happy shall you be, and it shall be well with you. Your wife shall be as a fruitful vine within your house: your children like be like olive plants around your table. Behold, thus shall the man be blessed who fears the Lord. (Ps 128:1-4)

In the fear of the Lord is the faithfulness of strength, and there shall be hope for his children. (Pro 14:26)

Which is the man who fears the Lord? He will teach them the way that they should choose. His soul will dwell upon good things, and his offspring will inherit the earth. (Ps 25:12-13)

Happy is the man who fears the Lord, who will delight in his commandments exceedingly. His offspring will be powerful on the earth. The generation of the upright will be blessed. Glory and wealth will be in his house, and his justice shall remain from age to age. (Ps 112:1-3)

Fear of God and healing (wellness)
The fear of the Lord will delight the heart, and will give joy and gladness and length of days. (Sir 1:12)

The fear of the Lord adds days. And the years of the impious will be shortened. (Pro 10:27)

The fear of the Lord is a fountain of life, so as to turn aside from the ruin of death. (Pro 14:27)

Fear of God helps us overcome sin
Moses said to the people: "Do not be afraid. For God came in order to test you, and so that the fear of him might be with you, and you would not sin." (Exo 20:20)

I will put my fear into their heart, so that they do not withdraw from me. (Jer 32:40)

By mercy and truth, iniquity is redeemed. And by the fear of the Lord, one turns away from evil. (Pro 16:6)

The eyes of the Lord are upon those who fear him. He is a powerful Protector, a Firmament of virtue, a Shelter from the heat, and a Covering from the midday sun, a Guardian from offenses, and a Helper from falling, who exalts the soul and illuminates the eyes, and who gives health and life and blessing. (Sir 34:19-20)

Moses said to the people: "Do not be afraid. For God came in order to test you, and so that the fear of him might be with you, and you would not sin." (Exo 20:20)

Fear of God brings spiritual gifts
The fear of the Lord is the beginning of wisdom. (Pro 1:7)

Fear of God keeps us protected
The fear of the Lord is unto life. And he shall linger in plentitude, without being visited by disaster. (Pro 19:23)

Fear of God takes away our shyness, timidity, and worldly fears
Those who fear the Lord will tremble at nothing, and they will not be terrified. For he is their hope. (Sir 34:16)

Fear of God fills us with hope
The spirit of those who fear God will live, for their hope is in him who saves them. (Sir 34:14-15)

Fear of God rescues us from troubles
No evils will befall one who fears the Lord. Instead, God will preserve him during temptation and will free him from evils. (Sir 33:1)

Fear of God brings financial blessings
The fruit of humility is the fear of the Lord, riches and glory and life. (Pro 22:4)

Fear the Lord, all you his holy ones. For there is no destitution for those who fear him. The rich have been needy and hungry, but those who seek the Lord will not be deprived of any good thing. (Ps 33:9-10)

How great is the multitude of your goodness, O Lord, which you have laid for those who fear you, which you have perfected for those who hope in you, in the sight of everyone. (Ps 31:19)

Fear of God helps us to be repentant
Whoever hates correction is walking in the steps of a sinner. But whoever fears God will convert within his heart. (Sir 21:6)

Fear of God will help us to praise God freely
You who fear the Lord, praise him. All the offspring of Jacob, glorify him. (Ps 22:23)

A person who is holy (fears God) will know and do the will of God
Which is the man who fears the Lord? He will teach them the way that they should choose. (Ps 25:12)

Fear of God helps us obey the commandments and love God
Those who fear the Lord will not be unbelieving toward his Word. And those who love him will keep to his way. Those who fear the Lord will seek the things that are well-pleasing to him. And those who love him will be filled with his law. (Sir 2:15-16)

Forgiveness

What are the blessings we receive when we forgive others?

Forgive others and God will forgive your sins
If you will forgive men their sins, your heavenly Father also will forgive you your offenses. But if you will not forgive men, neither will your Father forgive you your sins. (Matt 6:14-15)

When you stand to pray, if you hold anything against anyone, forgive them, so that your Father, who is in heaven, may also forgive you your sins. But if you will not forgive, neither will your Father, who is in heaven, forgive you your sins. (Mrk 11:25-26)

If one has no mercy toward another like himself, can he then seek pardon for his own sins? (Sir 28:4)

Forgive your neighbor, if he has harmed you, and then your sins will be forgiven you when you pray. (Sir 28:2)

Do not judge, and you will not be judged. Do not condemn, and you will not be condemned. Forgive, and you will be forgiven. (Luk 6:37)

Forgive others and God will hear your prayers
When you stand to pray, if you hold anything against anyone, forgive them. (Mrk 11:25)

Forgive your neighbor, if he has harmed you, and then your sins will be forgiven you when you pray. (Sir 28:2)

I want men to pray in every place, lifting up pure hands, without anger or dissension. (1 Tim 2:8)

If you offer your gift at the altar, and there you remember that your brother has something against you, leave your gift there, before the altar, and go first to be reconciled to your brother, and then you may approach and offer your gift. (Matt 5:23-24)

Forgive others and God will heal you
Forgive your neighbor, if he has harmed you, and then your sins will be forgiven you when you pray. A man holds on to anger against another man, and does he then expect healing from God? (Sir 28:2-3)

Forgiveness defeats Satan

Anyone whom you have forgiven of anything, I also forgive. And then, too, anyone I have forgiven, if I have forgiven anything, it was done in the person of Christ for your sakes, so that we would not be circumvented by Satan. For we are not ignorant of his intentions. (2 Cor 2:10-11)

Forgiveness frees us from bondages

Then his lord called him, and he said to him: 'You wicked servant, I forgave you all your debt, because you pleaded with me. Therefore, should you not also have had compassion on your fellow servant, just as I also had compassion on you?' And his lord, being angry, handed him over to the torturers, until he repaid the entire debt. So, too, shall my heavenly Father do to you, if each one of you will not forgive his brother from your hearts." (Matt 18:32-35)

Be reconciled with your adversary quickly, while you are still on the way with him, lest perhaps the adversary may hand you over to the judge, and the judge may hand you over to the officer, and you will be thrown in prison. Amen I say to you, that you shall not go forth from there, until you have repaid the last quarter. (Matt 5:25-26)

Forgiveness of sins

Prayer for forgiveness of sins

Help us, O God, our Savior. And free us, Lord, for the glory of your name. And forgive us our sins for the sake of your name. (Ps 79:9)

O God, be merciful to me, a sinner. (Luk 18:13)

O Lord, do not rebuke me in your fury, nor chastise me in your wrath. For your arrows have been driven into me, and your hand has been confirmed over me. (Ps 38:1-2)

Lord God, forgive, I beg you. (Amos 7:2)

Prayer for forgiveness of mortal sins
For your name's sake, O Lord, pardon my sin, for it is great. (Ps 25:11)

God's promise of forgiveness of our sins
I will forgive their iniquities, and I will no longer remember their sins. (Heb 8:12)

I will forgive their iniquity, and I will no longer remember their sin. (Jer 31:34)

I am. I am the very One who wipes away your iniquities for my own sake. And I will not remember your sins. (Is 43:25)

I have wiped away your iniquities like a cloud, and your sins like a mist. Return to me, because I have redeemed you. (Is 44:22)

Come now, let us argue it out, says the Lord. Then, if your sins are like scarlet, they shall be made white like snow; and if they are red like crimson, they shall become white like wool. (Is 1:18)

Fornication

God's warning for fornicators
Do you not know that wrongdoers will not possess the kingdom of God? Do not be deceived. For neither fornicators, nor idolaters, nor adulterers, nor the male prostitutes, nor sodomites, nor thieves, nor the greedy, nor the drunkard, nor slanderers, nor robbers shall possess the kingdom of God. (1 Cor 6:9-10)

Food is for the stomach, and the stomach is for food. But God shall destroy both the stomach and food. And the body is not for fornication, but rather for the Lord; and the Lord is for the body. (1 Cor 6:13)

Flee from fornication. Every sin whatsoever that a man commits is outside of the body, but whoever fornicates, sins against his own body. (1 Cor 6:18)

Know and understand this: no one who is a fornicator, or lustful, or one who is greedy holds an inheritance in the kingdom of Christ and of God. (Eph 5:5)

Fortitude, Strength

Word to meditate to be filled with the gift of fortitude
The Lord is my strength and my praise. And he has become my salvation. (Ps 118:14)

I can do all these things in him who strengthens me. (Phil 4:13)

It is he that gives power to the weary, and strengthens them that are powerless. Youths shall faint, and labor, and young men shall fall exhausted. But they that hope in the Lord shall renew their strength, they shall take wings as eagles, they shall run and not be weary, they shall walk and not faint. (Is 40:29-31)

Freedom

God's warning to those who abuse freedom
For you, brothers, have been called to freedom. Only you must not make freedom into an occasion for the flesh, but instead, serve one another through love. (Gal 5:13)

As servants of God, live as free people, yet do not use your freedom as a pretext for evil. (1 Pet 2:16)

For freedom Christ has set us free. Stand firm, and do not be willing to be again held by the yoke of slavery. (Gal 5:1)

Friendship

Prayer for protection from bad company (friendships)
Do not turn aside my heart to words of evil, to making excuses for sins, with men who work iniquity; and I will not communicate, and let me not eat of their delicacies. (Ps 141:4)

God's warning about sinful friendship
Be not deceived: evil company corrupt good manners. (1 Cor 15:33)

My son, if sinners should entice you, do not consent to them. (Pro 1:10)

Do not delight in the paths of the impious, nor permit the way of evil-doers to please you. Take flight from it. Do not pass close to it. Turn away and abandon it. For they do not sleep, unless they have done evil. And their sleep is quickly taken away from them, unless they have overthrown. (Pro 4:14-16)

God's promise for those who want to be freed from evil friendships
I will free you from hand of those who are most wicked, and I will redeem you from the hand of the powerful. (Jer 15:21)

Fruits of the Holy Spirit

God's promise of the fruits of the Holy Spirit
Whoever has received the seed into good soil, this is he who hears the word, and understands it, and so he bears fruit, and he produces: some a hundred fold, and another sixty fold, and another thirty fold. (Matt 13:23)

Every branch in me that does not bear fruit, he will take away. And each one that does bear fruit, he will cleanse, so that it may bring forth more fruit. (Jn 15:2)

What are the blessings we receive when we bear good fruits?

Our prayers will be answered

You have not chosen me, but I have chosen you. And I have appointed you, so that you may go forth and bear fruit, fruit that will last. Then whatever you have asked of the Father in my name, he will give to you. (Jn 15:16)

We become followers of Jesus

In this, my Father is glorified: that you should bear much fruit and become my disciples. (Jn 15:8)

We will be filled with more fruits

For whoever has, to him it shall be given more. And whoever has not, from him even what he has shall be taken away. (Mrk 4:25)

We enter into God's kingdom by producing the fruits of the Holy Spirit

Jesus said to them: "Have you never read in the Scriptures: 'The stone that the builders have rejected has become the cornerstone. By the Lord has this been done, and it is wonderful in our eyes? Therefore, I say to you, that the kingdom of God will be taken away from you, and it shall be given to a people who shall produce its fruits. (Matt 21:42-43)

God's warning to those who do not bear fruits

What more should I have done for my vineyard that I did not do for it? Should I not have expected it to produce grapes, though it produced wild vines? And now, I will reveal to you what I will do to my vineyard. I will take away its fence, and it will be plundered.

I will pull down its wall, and it will be trampled. And I will make it desolate. It will not be pruned, and it will not be dug. And briers and thorns will rise up. And I will command the clouds not to rain upon it. (Is 5:4-6)

Future

God's promise for our future
I know the plans that I have for you, said the Lord, plans for your welfare, and not for evil, to give you a future of hope. (Jer 29:11)

God's promise for those who worry about their future
Do not worry about tomorrow; for the future day will bring worries of its own. Today's trouble is enough for the day. (Matt 6:34)

G

Gambling

God's warning to gambling addicts
When an inheritance is obtained hastily in the beginning, in the end it will be without a blessing. (Pro 20:21)

Gift of Tongues

Word to meditate for those seeking to be blessed with the Gift of tongues
They were all filled with the Holy Spirit. And they began to speak in various languages, just as the Holy Spirit gave them ability. (Acts 2:4)

These signs will accompany those who believe. In my name, they shall cast out demons. They will speak in new languages. (Mrk 16:17)

God's Love

God's steadfast love
For the mountains will be moved, and the hills be removed. But my steadfast love will not depart from you.(Is 54:10)

The steadfast love of the Lord never ceases, his mercies will never come to an end. They are new every morning: great is your faithfulness. (Lam 3:22-23)

God's love for us even when we have committed a mortal sin
I am certain that neither death, nor life, nor Angels, nor Principalities, nor Powers, nor the present things, nor the future things, nor strength, nor the heights, nor the depths, nor any other

created thing, will be able to separate us from the love of God, which is in Christ Jesus our Lord. (Rom 8:38-39)

God's everlasting love for us

I have loved you with an everlasting love: therefore I have drawn you with my faithfulness. (Jer 31:3)

God's love for us even when we did not know him

God proves his love for us in that, while we were yet sinners, at the proper time, Christ died for us. (Rom 5:8)

God knows us by name (personal love)

Thus says the Lord who created you, O Jacob, and who formed you, O Israel: Do not be afraid. For I have redeemed you, and I have called you by your name. You are mine. (Is 43:1)

God's providential love for us

He will love you and multiply you. And he will bless the fruit of your womb, and the fruit of your land: your grain as well as your vintage, oil, and herds, and the flocks of your sheep, upon the land about which he swore to your fathers that he would give it to you. (Deut 7:13)

God's generous love for us

He who did not spare even his own Son, but handed him over for the sake of us all, will he not with him also give us everything else? (Rom 8:32)

God's motherly love

In the manner of one whom a mother comforts, so will I comfort you. And you will be comforted in Jerusalem. (Is 66:13)

God's marital love

For as the young man will live with the virgin, so shall your maker marry you. And the groom will rejoice over the bride, and your God will rejoice over you. (Is 62:5)

What are the blessings of being filled with God's love?

God's love is life giving

God, who is rich in mercy, for the sake of his exceedingly great love with which he loved us, even when we were dead in our sins, has enlivened us together in Christ, by whose grace you have been saved. (Eph 2:4-5)

The Lord, your God, is in your midst, a warrior who gives victory; he will rejoice over you with gladness, he will renew you in his love; he will exult over you with loud singing. (Zeph 3:17)

We are called God's Children

See how much of love the Father has given to us, that we would be called, and would become, the children of God. Because of this, the world does not know us, for it did not know God. (1 Jn 3:1)

We are saved from death and hell

Behold, the eye of the Lord is upon them that fear him, upon them that hope in his steadfast love; To deliver their soul from death, and to keep them alive in famine. (Ps 33:18-19)

Protection from evil

Many torments shall be to the wicked: but he who trusts in the Lord, steadfast love shall surround him. (Ps 32:10)

We are disciplined and corrected by God

My son, do not discard the discipline of the Lord, and do not fall away when you are corrected by him. For whomever the Lord loves, he corrects, and just as a father does with a son, he wins him over. (Pro 3:11-12)

My child, pay attention when the Lord corrects you, and do not lose heart when you are punished by him. For whomever the Lord loves, he chastises. And every child whom he accepts, he scourges.. (Heb 12:5-6)

Gluttony (Food Addiction)

Prayer for freedom from gluttony and lust
Lord, Father and God of my life. Do not leave me with the haughtiness of my eyes. And avert all evil desires from me. Let neither gluttony nor sexual desire take hold of me, and do not give me over to shameless passion. (Sir 23:5-6)

Word to Meditate
Whether you eat or drink, or whatever else you may do, do everything for the glory of God. (1 Cor 10:31)

Do not work for food that perishes, but for that which endures to eternal life, which the Son of man will give to you. (Jn 6:27)

Word to meditate for picky eaters
For every creature of God is good, and nothing is to be rejected which is received with thanksgiving; for it has been sanctified by the Word of God and by prayer. (1 Tim 4:4-5)

Gossip

Whoever hates gossip extinguishes evil. (Sir 19:6)

Whoever walks dishonestly reveals secrets. But whoever is of a faithful soul conceals what is confided by a friend. (Pro 11:13)

Do not become involved with him who reveals mysteries, and who walks deceitfully, and who enlarges his lips. (Pro 20:19)

Grace

What are the blessings of God's grace?

It is by grace that we are saved

For by grace, you have been saved through faith. And this is not your doing, for it is a gift of God. (Eph 2:8)

Yet still, God, who is rich in mercy, for the sake of his exceedingly great love with which he loved us, even when we were dead in our sins, has enlivened us together in Christ, by whose grace you have been saved. (Eph 2:4-5)

God's grace enables us to fulfill God's call

He said to me: "My grace is sufficient for you. For power is perfected in weakness." And so, willingly shall I glory in my weaknesses, so that the power of Christ may live within me. (2 Cor 12:9)

Greed

Watch out and guard yourselves from every kind of greed; for a person's life is not found in the abundance of the things that he possesses. (Luk 12:15)

No one is able to serve two masters. For either he will have hatred for the one, and love the other, or he will persevere with the one, and despise the other. You cannot serve God and wealth. (Matt 6:24)

Guilt

God's encouragement for those who experience guilt because of past sins

So if anyone is a new creation in Christ, what is old has passed away. Behold, all things have been made new. (2 Cor 5:17)

For God did not send his Son into the world, in order to judge the world, but in order that the world may be saved through him. Whoever believes in him is not judged. But whoever does not believe is already judged, because he does not believe in the name of the only-begotten Son of God. (Jn 3:17-18)

I will forgive their iniquities, and I will no longer remember their sins. (Heb 8:12)

I said, "I will confess against myself, my injustice to the Lord," and you forgave the guilt of my sin. (Ps 32:5)

Let us draw near with a true heart, in the fullness of faith, having hearts cleansed from an evil conscience, and bodies absolved with clean water. Let us hold fast to the confession of our hope, without wavering, for he who has promised is faithful. (Heb 10:22-23)

Prayer to free oneself from guilt
I have sinned exceedingly in doing this. I beg you take away the guilt of your servant. For I have acted unwisely. (1 Chron 21:8)

H

Hatred

If anyone says that he loves God, but hates his brother, then he is a liar. For he who does not love his brother, whom he does see, in what way can he love God, whom he does not see? (1 Jn 4:20)

Everyone who hates his brother is a murderer. And you know that no murderer has eternal life abiding within him. (1 Jn 3:15)

Hated by people

Prayer when we are hated by people
Have mercy upon me, O Lord; see my trouble which I suffer of them that hate me You have lifted me up from the gates of death, so that I may announce all your praises. (Ps 9:13)

Haughtiness

Pride goes before destruction and a haughty spirit before a fall. (Pro 16:18)

The heart of a man is haughty before it is crushed and humbled before it is glorified. (Pro 18:12)

Healing

God's promise of healing
In your infirmity, you should not neglect yourself, but pray to the Lord, and he will heal you. (Sir 38:9)

Is anyone ill among you? Let him bring in the priests of the Church, and let them pray over him, anointing him with oil in the name of the Lord. (Jas 5:14)

I saw his ways, and I healed him, and I led him back again, and I restored consolations to him and to those who mourn for him. I created the fruit of the lips: peace, peace to him who is far away, and peace to him who is near, said the Lord, and I healed him. (Is 57:18-19)

He himself was wounded because of our iniquities. He was bruised because of our wickedness. The discipline of our peace was upon him. And by his wounds, we are healed. (Is 53:5)

God's promise of healing of all kinds of diseases
When the sun had set, all those who had anyone afflicted with various diseases brought them to him. Then, laying his hands on each one of them, he cured them. (Luk 4:40)

Jesus traveled throughout all of the cities and towns, teaching in their synagogues, and preaching the Gospel of the kingdom, and healing every illness and every infirmity. (Matt 9:35)

The entire crowd was trying to touch him, because power went out from him and healed all. (Luk 6:19)

Bless the Lord, O my soul, and do not forget all his benefits. He forgives all your iniquities. He heals all your infirmities. (Ps 103:2-3)

A multitude also hurried to Jerusalem from the neighboring cities, carrying the sick and those troubled by unclean spirits, who were all healed. (Acts 5:16)

Many followed him, and he cured them all. (Matt 12:15)

Healing prayer for various sicknesses
Heal me, O Lord, and I will be healed. Save me, and I will be saved. For you are my praise. (Jer 17:14)

Healing prayer for incurable diseases (terminal sickness)
Lord, I will live for you, for you alone; Heal me and let me live. (Is 38:16,GNT)

Let me live and I will praise you, and let your ordinances assist me. (Ps 119:175)

Your hands have made me and formed me all around, and, in this way, do you suddenly throw me away? Remember that you have fashioned me like clay; and will you reduce me to dust? Have you not extracted me like milk and curdled me like cheese? You have clothed me with skin and flesh. You have put me together with bones and nerves. You have assigned to me life and mercy, and your visitation has preserved my spirit. (Job 10:8-12)

Turn to me, Lord, and save my life. Save me for the sake of your steadfast love. For there is no one in death who would be mindful of you. And who will praise to you in sheol? (Ps 6:4-5)

Healing prayer for skin diseases (Leprosy, Eczema, etc.)
Lord, if you are willing, you can cleanse me. (Matt 8:2)

Prayer of thanksgiving after surgery or healing from any sickness
O Lord my God, I cried to you for help, and you have healed me. O Lord, you brought up my soul from Sheol, restored me to life from among those gone down to the Pit. (Ps 30:1-2)

Healing prayer for physical pain
Have mercy on me, Lord, for I am languishing. Heal me, Lord, for my bones have become disturbed, and my soul has been very troubled. But as for you, Lord, how long? (Ps 6:2-3)

Healing prayer for blindness
Consider and hear me, O Lord my God: lighten my eyes, or I will sleep the sleep of death. (Ps 13:3)

Lord, let me see again. (Luk 18:41)

God's promise for those who are blind
I will lead the blind along a way which they do not know. And I will cause them to walk along paths with which they were unfamiliar. I will turn darkness into light before them, and crooked into straight. These things I have done for them. For I have not abandoned them. (Is 42:16)

God's promise for people with incurable diseases
Behold, I will lead over them recovery and health, and I will cure them. And I will reveal to them an abundance of prosperity and security. (Jer 33:6)

God's promise for those with muscle, joints ache such as Arthritis, Fibromyalgia)
I can do all things through Christ who strengthens me. (Phil 4:13)

God's promise for those who are bedridden
But unto you, who fear my name, the Sun of justice will arise, and health will be in his wings. And you will go forth and leap like the calves of the herd. (Mal 4:2)

The Lord will sustain them upon their sickbed. In their illness you heal all their infirmities. (Ps 41:3)

God's promise for people with stammering speech
The tongue of those with stammering speech will speak quickly and plainly. (Is 32:5)

God's promise for people in coma
If the Spirit of him who raised up Jesus from the dead lives within you, then he who raised up Jesus Christ from the dead will also give life to your mortal bodies, by means of his Spirit living within you. (Rom 8:11)

Blessing prayer of healing over others
Beloved, concerning everything, I make it my prayer that all may go well with you and that you may be in good health as with your soul. (3 Jn 1:2)

Prayer for God's mercy when you have heard a negative word from your doctor about your health
I beg you, Lord, I beseech you, to remember how I walked before you in truth and with a whole heart, and that I have done what is good in your sight. (Is 38:3)

God's promise for a terminally ill child
There will no longer be an infant who lives only a few days, nor an elder who does not complete his days. for one who dies at a hundred years will be considered a youth . (Is 65:20)

Heart

For from within, from the heart of men, come evil thoughts which lead you to do immoral things, to rob, kill, commit adultery, be greedy, and do all sorts of evil things; deceit, fornication, envy, slander, pride, and folly — all these evil things come from inside you and make you unclean. (Mrk 7:21-23)

How are you able to speak good things while you are evil? For out of the abundance of the heart, the mouth speaks. A good person brings good things from a good treasure. And an evil person brings evil things from an evil treasure. (Matt 12:34-35)

Heaven

God's promise for our heavenly life
For behold, I am about to create the new heavens and the new earth. And the former things will not be in memory and will not enter into the heart. But you will be glad and exult, even forever, in these things that I create. For behold, I create Jerusalem as an exultation, and its people as a joy. (Is 65:17-18)

In my Father's house, there are many dwelling places. If there were not so, would I have told you that I go to prepare a place for you. And if I go and prepare a place for you, I will return again, and then I will take you to myself, so that where I am, you also may be. (Jn 14:2-3)

Help

Prayer of blessing over someone who has helped you
May you be blessed by the Lord. For you have shown me compassion. (1 Sam 23:21)

God's promise for those who need help with various things
Fear not. I will help you, says the Lord, your Redeemer, the Holy One of Israel. (Is 41:14)

I have lifted up my eyes to the mountains; from where will help come to me. My help is from the Lord, who made heaven and earth. (Ps 121:1-2)

Holiness

God's promise for those who live a godly, holy, righteous life
The Lord God is a sun and shield; He will not withhold good things from those who walk uprightly. O Lord of hosts, blessed is the man who hopes in you. (Ps 84:11-12)

Holy Spirit

God's promise of the Holy Spirit

After this, it will happen that I will pour out my spirit upon all flesh, and your sons and your daughters will prophesy; your elders will dream dreams, and your youths will see visions. Moreover, in those days I will pour out my spirit upon my servants and handmaids. (Joel 2:28-29)

All who drink from this water will thirst again. But whoever shall drink from the water that I will give to him will not thirst for eternity. Instead, the water that I will give to him will become in him a fountain of water, springing up into eternal life. (Jn 4:13-14)

I will pour out waters upon the thirsty ground, and rivers upon the dry land. I will pour out my Spirit upon your descendants, and my blessing upon your offspring. (Is 44:3)

Let anyone who thirsts, come unto me, and He that believes in me, let him drink. As the scripture has said, 'out of the believers heart shall flow rivers of living water.' (Jn 7:37-38)

Ask, and it shall be given to you. Seek, and you shall find. Knock, and it shall be opened to you. For everyone who asks, receives; and whoever seeks, finds; and to anyone who knocks, it will be opened. (Matt 7:7-8)

In that day, there will be a fountain open to the house of David and to the inhabitants of Jerusalem, o cleanse them from sin and impurity. (Zech 13:1)

The waters have burst forth in the desert, and fountains in solitary places. And the wilderness will have a pool of water, and the thirsty land will have springs of water. (Is 35:6-7)

I will open rivers in the high hills, and fountains in the midst of the plains. I will turn the desert into pools of water, and the impassable land into streams of water. (Is 41:18)

God's promise of the Holy Spirit for those who minister
You shall receive power when the Holy Spirit has come over you, and you shall be witnesses for me in Jerusalem, and in all Judea and Samaria, and even to the ends of the earth. (Acts 1:8)

What are the blessings we receive when we are filled with the Holy Spirit?
The Holy Spirit helps us with prayer (intercessor)
The Spirit also helps our weakness. For we do not know how to pray as we ought, but the Spirit himself asks on our behalf with sighs too deep for words. And he who examines hearts knows what the Spirit seeks, because he asks on behalf of the saints in accordance with God. (Rom 8:26-27)

The Holy Spirit helps us to praise and worship God
The wild beasts of the field will glorify me, with the serpents and the ostriches. For I have brought waters to the desert, rivers to the desert, in order to give drink to my people, to my elect. This is the people whom I have formed for myself. They will speak my praise. (Is 43:20-21)

The Holy Spirit is our Guide (leads us)
You gave them your good Spirit, so that he might teach them. (Neh 9:20)

For if you live according to the flesh, you will die. But if, by the Spirit, you mortify the deeds of the flesh, you shall live. For all those who are led by the Spirit of God are the sons of God. (Rom 8:13-14)

Teach me to do your will. For you are my God. Your good Spirit will lead me into the righteous land. (Ps 143:10)

If we live by the Spirit, we should also be guided by the Spirit. (Gal 5:25)

He makes us holy and spiritual

You are not in the flesh, but in the spirit, if it is true that the Spirit of God lives within you. But if anyone does not have the Spirit of Christ, he does not belong to him. (Rom 8:9)

He teaches us

As for you, let the Anointing that you have received from him abide in you. And so, you have no need of anyone to teach you. For his Anointing teaches you about everything, and it is the truth, and it is not a lie. And just as his Anointing has taught you, abide in him. (1 Jn 2:27)

He shall glorify me. For he will receive from what is mine, and he will announce it to you. All things whatsoever that the Father has are mine. For this reason, I said that he will receive from what is mine and that he will announce it to you. (Jn 16:14-15)

I still have many things to say to you, but you are not able to bear them now. But when the Spirit of truth has arrived, he will teach the whole truth to you. For he will not be speaking from himself. Instead, whatever he will hear, he will speak. And he will announce to you the things that are to come. (Jn 16:12-13)

He helps us worship Jesus

I would have you know that no one speaking in the Spirit of God utters a curse against Jesus. And no one is able to say that Jesus is Lord, except in the Holy Spirit. (1 Cor 12:3)

He reminds us all that we must know

But the Advocate, the Holy Spirit, whom the Father will send in my name, will teach you all things and will remind you everything whatsoever that I have said to you. (Jn 14:26)

When he comes, he will prove the world wrong about sin and righteousness and judgment: about sin, because they have not believed in me; about righteousness, because I am going to the Father, and you will not see me any longer; about judgment, because the ruler of this world has already been condemned. (Jn 16:8-11)

He fills us with power to live our Christian lives
You shall receive power when the Holy Spirit has come over you, and you shall be witnesses for me in Jerusalem, and in all Judea and Samaria, and even to the ends of the earth. (Acts 1:8)

He is our advocate (paraclete)
Nevertheless I tell you the truth: it is to your advantage that I go away, for if I do not go away, the Advocate will not come to you; but if I go, I will send him to you. (Jn 16:7)

He reveals to us things that are to come
When the Spirit of truth comes, he will teach the whole truth to you. For he will not be speaking from himself. Instead, whatever he will hear, he will speak. And he will announce to you the things that are to come. (Jn 16:13)

He gives us inner strength
I pray that he would grant you, according to the riches of his glory, to be strengthened with power by his Spirit in your inner being. (Eph 3:16)

The Holy Spirit is given to us to do God's work
The Spirit of the Lord is upon me, for the Lord has anointed me. He has sent me to bring good news to the meek, so as to heal the contrite of heart, to preach leniency to captives and release to the confined, and so to proclaim the acceptable year of the Lord and the day of vindication of our God: to console all who are mourning. (Is 61:1-2)

He whom God has sent speaks the words of God. for he gives the Spirit without measure. (Jn 3:34)

The Holy Spirit gives us power to do God's work
You shall receive power when the Holy Spirit, has come over you, and you shall be witnesses for me in Jerusalem, and in all Judea and Samaria, and even to the ends of the earth. (Acts 1:8)

When they hand you over, do not choose to think about how or what to speak. For what to speak shall be given to you in that hour. For it is not you who will be speaking, but the Spirit of your Father, who will speak in you. (Matt 10:19-20)

The Spirit of the Lord speaks through me, and his word is spoken through my tongue. (2 Sam 23:2)

He fills our thirst (Emptiness)
If anyone thirsts, let him come to me and drink (Jn 7:37)

Whoever shall drink from the water that I will give to him will not thirst for eternity. Instead, the water that I will give to him will become in him a fountain of water, springing up into eternal life. (Jn 4:14)

The Holy Spirit will help us obey God's law
I will place my Spirit within you. And I will make you walk in my precepts and keep my judgments. (Eze 36:27)

If you are led by the Spirit, you are not under the law. (Gal 5:18)

The Holy Spirit reveals the will of God to us
Who will know your mind, unless you give them wisdom and send your holy spirit from on high? (Wis 9:17)

The Holy Spirit cleanses us
The Lord will have washed away the filth of the daughters of Zion, and will have washed away the blood of Jerusalem from its midst, by means of a spirit of judgment and a spirit of burning. And the Lord will create, over every place of Mount Zion and wherever he is called upon, a cloud by day and a smoke with the splendor of burning fire by night. (Is 4:4-5)

The Holy Spirit delivers us from evil
If I cast out demons by the Spirit of God, then the kingdom of God has arrived among you. (Matt 12:28)

The Holy Spirit makes us intimate with God
In this way, we know that we abide in him, and he in us: because he has given to us from his Spirit. (1 Jn 4:13)

The Holy Spirit fills us with God's love
God's love is poured forth in our hearts through the Holy Spirit that has been given to us. (Rom 5:5)

The Holy Spirit keeps us interested in spiritual matters
Those who are in agreement with the flesh are mindful of the things of the flesh. But those who are in agreement with the spirit are mindful of the things of the spirit. (Rom 8:5)

The Holy Spirit helps us fight and overcome sin and temptation
Jesus was led by the Spirit into the desert, in order to be tempted by the devil. (Matt 4:1)

The Holy Spirit transforms us into the image and likeness of Jesus
Truly, all of us, as we gaze upon the unveiled glory of the face of the Lord, are transfigured into the same image, from one glory to another. And this is done by the Spirit of the Lord. (2 Cor 3:18)

The Holy Spirit helps us understand Godly (spiritual) matters

We have not received the spirit of this world, but the Spirit who is of God, so that we may understand the things that have been given to us by God. (1 Cor 2:12)

The Spirit of Truth, whom the world cannot receive, because it neither perceives him nor knows him. But you shall know him. For he will remain with you, and he will be in you. (Jn 14:17)

The Holy Spirit convicts us of sin

When he will come, he will prove the world wrong about sin, and of righteousness, and of judgment. (Jn 16:8)

The Holy Spirit gives us life (He is the life giver)

If the Spirit of him who raised up Jesus from the dead lives within you, then he who raised up Jesus Christ from the dead shall also enliven your mortal bodies, by means of his Spirit living within you. (Rom 8:11)

If you live according to the flesh, you will die. But if, by the Spirit, you mortify the deeds of the flesh, you shall live. (Rom 8:13)

Whatever a man will have sown, that also shall he reap. For whoever sows in his flesh, from the flesh he shall also reap corruption. But whoever sows in the Spirit, from the Spirit he shall reap eternal life. (Gal 6:8)

The Holy Spirit fills us with the presence of God

In this way, we know that we abide in him, and he in us: because he has given to us from his Spirit. (1 Jn 4:13)

Those who keep his commandments abide in him, and he in them. And we know that he abides in us by this: by the Spirit, whom he has given to us. (1 Jn 3:24)

The Holy Spirit unites us with all believers
Indeed, in one Spirit, we were all baptized into one body, whether Jews or Gentiles, whether servant or free. And we all drank in the one Spirit. (1 Cor 12:13)

The Holy Spirit increases our faith in Jesus
No one speaking in the Spirit of God utters a curse against Jesus. And no one is able to say that Jesus is Lord, except in the Holy Spirit. (1 Cor 12:3)

But you, most beloved, are building yourselves up by your most holy faith, praying in the Holy Spirit. (Jude 1:20)

The Holy Spirit will teach us God's Word
Understand this first: that every prophecy of Scripture does not result from one's own interpretation. For prophecy was not conveyed by human will at any time. Instead, holy men were speaking about God while inspired by the Holy Spirit. (2 Pet 1:20-21)

The eye has not seen, and the ear has not heard, nor has it entered into the heart of man, what things God has prepared for those who love him." But God has revealed these things to us through his Spirit. For the Spirit searches all things, even the depths of God. (1 Cor 2:9-10)

The Holy Spirit will fill us with Charisms
I will pour out my spirit upon all flesh, and your sons and your daughters will prophesy; your elders will dream dreams, and your youths will see visions. (Joel 2:28)

The Holy Spirit will perform signs and wonders in our lives
In those days I will pour out my spirit upon my servants and handmaids. And I will grant wonders in the sky and on earth: blood and fire and the vapor of smoke. (Joel 2:29-30)

He stays in our family line and also helps our descendants

This is my covenant with them, says the Lord. My Spirit is within you, and my words, which I have put in your mouth, will not withdraw from your mouth, nor from the mouth of your offspring, nor from the mouth of your offspring's offspring, says the Lord, from this moment, and even forever. (Is 59:21)

The Holy Spirit gives us rest (body, mind, and soul)

Like an animal who descends to an open field, the Spirit of the Lord gave them rest. Thus did you lead your people, in order to make a glorious name for yourself. (Is 63:14)

Home

God's promise for those buying or building a house

Unless the Lord has built the house, those who build it have labored in vain. Unless the Lord has guarded the city, he who guards it watches in vain. (Ps 127:1)

God's promise for those who are looking for a bigger home

Enlarge the place of your tent and extend the curtains of your habitations, unsparingly. Lengthen your cords, and strengthen your stakes. For you shall extend to the right and to the left. And your offspring shall inherit the nations, and you shall inhabit the desolate cities. (Is 54:1-2)

God's promise for those living in rented homes

I have given a place to my people Israel. They shall be planted, and they shall live in it, and they shall no longer be moved. (1 Chron 17:9)

They will build houses, and will inhabit them. And they will plant vineyards, and will eat their fruits. (Is 65:21)

Blessing prayer for new homes

Look with favor from your sanctuary and from your lofty habitation amid the heavens, and bless your people Israel and the land which you have given to us, just as you swore to our fathers, a land flowing with milk and honey. (Deut 26:15)

God's promise for our homes when we praise him

Sing praise and rejoice, daughter of Zion. For behold, I come, and I will dwell in your midst, says the Lord. (Zech 2:10)

Praise the Lord, O Jerusalem. Praise your God, O Zion. For he has reinforced the bars of your gates. He has blessed your children within you. He has stationed peace at your borders, and he has satisfied you with the fat of the grain. (Ps 147:12-14)

God's promise of protection for our home

The Lord is your keeper, the Lord is your protection, at your right hand. The sun will not burn you by day, nor the moon by night. The Lord guards you from all evil. May the Lord guard your soul. May the Lord guard your entrance and your exit, from this time forward and even forever. (Ps 121:5-8)

Like birds flying overhead, so will the Lord of hosts protect Jerusalem, protecting and freeing, passing over and saving it. (Is 31:5)

Because you have made the Lord, your refuge, the most High, your dwelling place; No evil befall you, neither shall any scourge come near your dwelling. (Ps 91:9-10)

Prayer to bless the home

Bless the house of your servant, so that it may be forever before you. For you, O Lord God, have spoken. And so, let the house of your servant be blessed with your blessing forever. (2 Sam 7:29)

Let it please you to bless the house of your servant, so that it may be always before you. For since it is you who is blessing, O Lord, it shall be blessed forever. (1 Chron 17:27)

Prayer when the house is being taken away (Foreclosure, unable to pay mortgage)
Look with favor upon the prayer of your servant and upon his petitions, O Lord, my God. Listen to the cry and the prayer, which your servant prays before you this day, so that your eyes may be open over this house, night and day, over the house about which you said, 'My name shall be there,' so that you may heed the prayer that your servant is praying in this place to you. (1 Kgs 8:28-29)

My dwelling has been taken away; it has been folded up and taken from me, like the tent of a shepherd. My life has been cut off, as if by a weaver. While I was still beginning, he cut me off. From morning until evening, you have marked out my limits. (Is 38:12-13)

God's promise for those whose homes are infested with rodents and other creatures
I will make a covenant of peace with them. And I will banish the harmful beasts from the land. And those who are living in the wild will sleep securely. And I will make them a blessing all around my hill. (Eze 34:25-26)

Homeless

God's promise for those who are homeless
God gives the desolate a home to live in; he leads out the prisoners to prosperity. (Ps 68:6, NRSVCE)

They will not hunger or thirst, nor will the heat of the sun beat down upon them. For the one who takes pity on them will lead them, and he will give them to drink from fountains of waters. (Is 49:10)

Honesty

God's promise for those who are honest

You shall not have differing weights, greater and lesser, in your bag. Neither shall there be in your house a greater and a lesser measure. You shall have a just and a true weight, and your measure shall be equal and true, so that you may live for a long time upon the land, which the Lord your God will give to you. (Deut 25:14-16)

Do not choose to be anxious for dishonest wealth. For these things will not benefit you in the day of darkness and retribution. (Sir 5:8)

Hope

Let your heart be strengthened, all you who hope in the Lord. (Ps 31:24)

For we have been saved by hope. But a hope which is seen is not hope. For when a man sees something, why would he hope? But since we hope for what we do not see, we wait for it with patience. (Rom 8:24-25)

Humility

What are the Blessings we receive for being humble?

A humble person is Exalted by God

Be humbled in the sight of the Lord, and he will exalt you. (Jas 4:10)

Be humbled under the powerful hand of God, so that he may exalt you in the time of visitation. (1 Pet 5:6)

Whoever has exalted himself, shall be humbled. And whoever has humbled himself, shall be exalted. (Matt 23:12)

Gift of wisdom
When pride comes, then comes disgrace; but wisdom is with the humble. (Pro 11:2)

God hears the prayer of a humble person
The prayer of one who humbles himself will pierce the clouds. And it will not be consoled until it draws near; and it will not withdraw until the Most High beholds. (Sir 35:21)

Your heart was penitent, and you humbled yourself in the sight of God concerning these things which have been said against this place and against the inhabitants of Jerusalem, and since, revering my face, you have torn your garments, and have wept before me: I also have heeded you, says the Lord. (2 Chron 34:27)

A humble person will receive graces from God
Perform your works in meekness, and you shall be loved beyond the glory of men. However great you may be, humble yourself in all things, and you will find grace in the presence of God. (Sir 3:17-18)

God resists the proud, but he gives grace to the humble. (Jas 4:6)

A humble person will receive God's favor
The fruit of humility is the fear of the Lord, riches and glory and life. (Pro 22:4)

For the Lord is exalted, and he looks with favor on the humble. But the lofty he knows from a distance. (Ps 138:6)

God delights in working with a humble person
The Lord is well pleased with his people, and he will exalt the humble unto salvation. (Ps 149:4)

He will direct the mild in judgment. He will teach the meek his ways. (Ps 25:9)

We receive forgiveness of sins when we are humble
If my people, over whom my name has been invoked, humble themselves, and pray and seek my face and turn from their wicked ways, then I will heed them from heaven, and I will forgive their sins, and I will heal their land. (2 Chron 7:14)

We receive God's mercy when we are humble
For, to the little, great mercy is granted, but the powerful will endure powerful torment. (Wis 6:6)

Yet truly, because they were humbled, the wrath of the Lord turned away from them, and so they were not utterly destroyed. (2 Chron 12:12)

God delivers a humble person from all evil and dangers
For you will deliver the humble people, but you will bring down the eyes of the arrogant. (Ps 18:27)

When the Lord had seen that they were humbled, the word of the Lord came to Shemaiah, saying: "Because they have been humbled, I will not disperse them. And I will give to them a little help, and my fury will not rain down upon Jerusalem. (2 Chron 12:7)

God reveals his will to a humble person
He will direct the humble in what is right. He will teach the meek his ways. (Ps 25:9)

God watches over a humble person
My hand has made all these things, and all these things have been made, says the Lord. But upon whom will I look with favor, except upon a humble person, who is contrite in spirit, and who trembles at my word? (Is 66:2)

Hunger & Thirst

God's promise for those who are poor and hungry

Blessed are you poor, for yours is the kingdom of God. Blessed are you who are hungry now, for you shall be satisfied. Blessed are you who are weeping now, for you shall laugh. (Luk 6:20-21)

He has satisfied the thirsty, and he has satisfied the hungry soul with good things. (Ps 107:9)

You will eat with enjoyment, and you will be satisfied, and you will praise the name of the Lord your God, who has worked miracles with you. (Joel 2:26)

They did not thirst in the desert, when he led them out. He produced water from the rock for them. For he split the rock, and the waters flowed out. (Is 48:21)

Husband

God's advice to the husbands

A husband should fulfill his obligation to his wife, and a wife should also act similarly toward her husband. (1 Cor 7:3)

It is not the wife, but the husband, who has power over her body. But, similarly also, it is not the husband, but the wife, who has power over his body. (1 Cor 7:4)

Do not fail in your obligations to one another, except perhaps by consent, for a limited time, so that you may empty yourselves for prayer. And then, return together again, lest Satan tempt you by means of your abstinence. (1 Cor 7:5)

I

Identity (Self-identity)

God's Word about who we are

I am a child of God

The Spirit himself renders testimony to our spirit that we are children of God. (Rom 8:16)

I am blessed

He blessed them, saying: "Increase and multiply, and fill the waters of the sea. And let the birds be multiplied above the land." (Gen 1:22)

God blessed them, and he said, "Increase and multiply, and fill the earth, and subdue it, and have dominion over the fish of the sea, and the flying creatures of the air, and over every living thing that moves upon the earth." (Gen 1:28)

Blessed be the God and Father of our Lord Jesus Christ, who has blessed us with every spiritual blessing in the heavens, in Christ. (Eph 1:3)

I am chosen

You are a holy people to the Lord your God. The Lord your God has chosen you so that you would be his particular people out of all the peoples who are upon the earth. (Deut 7:6)

You are a holy people, for the Lord your God. And he chose you, so that you may be a people particularly his, out of all the nations on earth. (Deut 14:2)

Today, the Lord has chosen you, so that you may be his particular people, just as he has spoken to you, and so that you may keep all his precepts. (Deut 26:18)

I am a royal priest
You are a chosen generation, a royal priesthood, a holy nation, an acquired people, so that you may proclaim the mighty acts of him who has called you out of darkness into his marvelous light. (1 Pet 2:9)

I am the salt of the Earth
You are the salt of the earth. (Matt 5:13)

I am the Light of the world
You are the light of the world. (Matt 5:14)

I am precious to God
Because you are precious and honorable in my eyes, I have loved you, and I will present men on behalf of you, and nations on behalf of your life. (Is 43:4)

If, therefore, you will hear my voice, and you will keep my covenant, you will be to me a treasured possession out of all people. For all the earth is mine. And you will be to me a priestly kingdom and a holy nation. (Exo 19:5-6)

I am wonderfully made
I praise you, for I am fearfully and wonderfully made. Wonderful are your works. (Ps 139:14)

God has a plan for me
I know the plans that I have for you, says the Lord, plans of your welfare, and not for evil, to give you a future of hope. (Jer 29:11)

All things work together for my Good
We know that all things work together unto good, for those who love God, who are called in accordance with his purpose. (Rom 8:28)

I can do all things
I can do all things in him who strengthens me. (Phil 4:13)

God loves me
I have loved you with an everlasting love: therefore I have drawn you with my faithfulness. (Jer 31:3)

I belong to God
You shall be holy unto me, because I, the Lord, am holy, and I have separated you from the other peoples, so that you would be mine. (Lev 20:26)

All the peoples of the earth shall see that the name of the Lord has been invoked over you, and they shall fear you. (Deut 28:10)

I am strong
Let the weak say, 'I am strong.' (Joel 3:10)

Idol Worship

How can Idolatry and Idol worship block and rob our blessings?
I am the Lord your God. You shall not make for yourselves an idol or a graven image. Neither shall you erect a monument, or set up a conspicuous stone in your land, in order that you may adore it. For I am the Lord your God. (Lev 26:1)

They have served foreign gods, and adored them, though they did not know them, and though they had not been allotted to them. For this reason, the fury of the Lord was enraged against this land, so as to lead over it all the curses which have been written in this book. (Deut 29:26-27)

Immigrant, Immigration

Prayer of blessing over a person needing help with immigration
May he give the blessings of Abraham to you, and to your offspring after you, so that you may possess the land where you now live as an alien (Gen 28:4)

God's promise for those who have applied for immigration
Trust in the Lord and do good, so you will live in the land, and so you shall enjoy security. Delight in the Lord, and he will grant to you the desires of your heart. (Ps 37:3-4)

Prayer for people living in Non-Christian countries
O Lord our God, other lords have ruled over us apart from you, but we acknowledge your name alone. (Is 26:13)

Inner Healing (Healing of soul, mind, memories, emotions, thoughts)

God's promise of inner healing
I will close up your scar, and I will heal you of your wounds, says the Lord. (Jer 30:17)

He heals the broken of heart, and he binds up their wounds. (Ps 147:3)

He himself was wounded because of our iniquities. He was bruised because of our wickedness. The discipline of our peace was upon him. And by his wounds, we are healed. (Is 53:5)

The light of the moon will be like the light of the sun, and the light of the sun will be sevenfold, like the light of seven days, in the day when the Lord will bind the wound of his people, and when he will heal the stroke of their scourge. (Is 30:26)

Prayer for healing of emotions

How long, O Lord? Will you forget me until the end? How long will you turn your face away from me? How long must I bear pain in my soul, and have sorrow in my heart throughout the day? (Ps 13:1-2)

Prayer for healing of the soul

Lord, be merciful unto me: heal my soul; for I have sinned against you. (Ps 41:4)

Prayer for inner healing

I have been altogether afflicted, Lord. Revive me according to your word. (Ps 119:107)

But as for you, Lord, O Lord: act on my behalf for your name's sake. For your mercy is sweet. Free me, for I am destitute and poor, and my heart has been disquieted within me. (Ps 109:21-22)

Intercession

Blessings we receive when we intercede for others
We will be materially blessed
The Lord restored the fortunes of Job, when he prayed for his friends. And the Lord gave to Job twice as much as he had before. (Job 42:10)

We will receive the power of the Holy Spirit
There was a man in Jerusalem, whose name was Simeon, and this man was righteous and devout, looking for the consolation of Israel, and the Holy Spirit was upon him. (Luk 2:25, RSVCE)

Intercessory prayers

Prayer for God's mercy on those who are victims of our sin
It is I who sinned; it is I who did evil. This flock, what does it deserve? O Lord my God, I beg you to let your hand be turned

against me and against the house of my father. But let not your people be struck down. (1 Chron 21:17)

Insult

Prayer

You know me, O Lord. Remember me, and visit me, and watch over me, because of those who persecute me. In your patience, do not choose to let me endure. You know I have suffered insult because of you. (Jer 15:15)

Interview

God's promise for those attending interview

Do not worry about how or what to speak. For what to speak shall be given to you in that hour. For it is not you who will be speaking, but the Spirit of your Father, who will speak through you. (Matt 10:19-20)

Prayer of an interviewer who must choose a candidate

May you, O Lord, who knows the heart of everyone, reveal which one of these you have chosen. (Acts 1:24)

J

Jealousy

God's warning against the sin of jealousy
For where there is jealousy and selfish ambition, there will be disorder and every vile practice. (Jas 3:16)

Jealousy and anger will diminish your days, and anxiety will bring old age before its time. A cheerful and good heart is like a feast. And its feasts are formed by diligence. (Sir 30:24-25)

Jesus

What are the blessings we receive for believing in Jesus?
Eternal life
I say to you, that whoever hears my word, and believes in him who sent me, has eternal life, and he does not go into judgment, but instead he crosses from death into life. (Jn 5:24)

Whoever believes in the Son has eternal life, but whoever rejects the Son will not see life, for God's wrath remains on them. (Jn 3:36)

For God so loved the world that he gave his only-begotten Son, so that all who believe in him may not perish, but may have eternal life. (Jn 3:16)

In my Father's house, there are many dwelling places. If there were not so, would I have told you that I go to prepare a place for you. And if I go and prepare a place for you, I will return again, and then I will take you to myself, so that where I am, you also may be. (Jn 14:2-3)

Whoever believes in him is not condemned. But whoever does not believe is already condemned, because he does not believe in the name of the only begotten Son of God. (Jn 3:18)

Amen, amen, I say to you, whoever believes in me has eternal life. (Jn 6:47)

My sheep hear my voice. And I know them, and they follow me. And I give them eternal life, and they shall never perish. And no one shall seize them from my hand. (Jn 10:27-28)

Blessed be the God and Father of our Lord Jesus Christ, who according to his great mercy has regenerated us into a living hope, through the resurrection of Jesus Christ from the dead: unto an incorruptible and undefiled and unfading inheritance, which is reserved for you in heaven. (1 Pet 1:3-4)

Life in this world
You study the Scriptures for you think that in them you have eternal life. And yet they also offer testimony about me. And you are not willing to come to me, so that you may have life. (Jn 5:39-40)

Your ancestors ate manna in the desert, and they died. This is the bread which descends from heaven, so that if anyone will eat from it, he may not die. (Jn 6:49-50)

You know the grace of our Lord Jesus Christ, that though he was rich, he became poor for your sakes, so that through his poverty, you might become rich. (2 Cor 8:9)

We become the children of God
Whoever did accept him, those who believed in his name, he gave them the power to become children of God. These are born, not of

blood, nor of the will of flesh, nor of the will of man, but of God. (Jn 1:12-13)

When the fullness of time arrived, God sent his Son, formed from a woman, formed under the law, so that he might redeem those who were under the law, in order that we might receive adoption as children. (Gal 4:4-5)

We become new creation
If anyone is in Christ, there is a new creation, everything old has passed away. Behold, all things have been made new. (2 Cor 5:17)

Our sins are forgiven
To him all the Prophets offer testimony that through his name all who believe in him receive forgiveness of sins. (Acts 10:43)

In this is love: not as if we had loved God, but that he first loved us, and so he sent his Son as the atoning sacrifice for our sins. (1 Jn 4:10)

He has rescued us from the power of darkness, and he has transferred us into the kingdom of his beloved son, in whom we have redemption, the forgiveness of sins. (Col 1:13-14)

Freedom from sin and addictions
By this Jesus everyone who believes is set free from all those sins from which you could not be freed by the law of Moses. (Acts 13:39)

If the Son makes you free, you will be free indeed. (Jn 8:36)

Freedom from curses
Christ has redeemed us from the curse of the law, since he became a curse for us. For it is written: "Cursed is anyone who hangs from a tree." (Gal 3:13)

Salvation of our souls

I am the gate. Those who come in through me will be saved. They will come and go freely and will find good pastures. (Jn 10:9, NLT)

The saying is trustworthy, and worthy of acceptance by everyone, that Christ Jesus came into this world to bring salvation to sinners, among whom I am the foremost. (1 Tim 1:15)

He will free the poor from the powerful, and the poor one who has no helper. He will spare the poor and the indigent, and he will bring salvation to the souls of the poor. He will redeem their souls from oppression and from iniquity, and their names shall be honorable in his sight. (Ps 72:12-14)

The Son of man has come to seek and to save what had been lost. (Luk 19:10)

Salvation of our families

Believe on the Lord Jesus, and you will be saved, you and your household. (Acts 16:31)

If you confess with your mouth the Lord Jesus, and if you believe in your heart that God has raised him up from the dead, you shall be saved. (Rom 10:9)

Abundant life

The thief comes, only so that he may steal and kill and destroy. I have come so that they may have life, and have it more abundantly. (Jn 10:10)

Whoever would save his life, will lose it. But whoever will have lost his life for my sake, shall find it. (Matt 16:24-25)

I am the good Shepherd. The good Shepherd gives his life for his sheep. (Jn 10:11)

Whoever has the Son, has Life. Whoever does not have the Son, does not have Life. (1 Jn 5:12)

We receive the Holy Spirit

If you knew the gift of God, and who it is who is saying to you, 'Give me to drink,' perhaps you would have made a request of him, and he would have given you living water. (Jn 4:10)

If anyone thirsts, let him come to me and drink: whoever believes in me, just as Scripture says, 'Out of the believer's heart shall flow rivers of living water.' Now he said this about the Spirit, which those who believe in him would soon be receiving. (Jn 7:37-39)

God poured out the Holy Spirit abundantly on us through Jesus Christ our Savior, so that by his grace we might be put right with God and come into possession of the eternal life we hope for. (Tit 3:6-7, GNT)

Therefore, being exalted to the right hand of God, and having received from the Father the Promise of the Holy Spirit, he poured this out, just as you now see and hear. (Acts 2:33)

We receive resurrection of life

I descended from heaven, not to do my own will, but the will of him who sent me. Yet this is the will of the Father who sent me: that I should lose nothing out of all that he has given to me, but that I should raise them up on the last day. (Jn 6:38-39)

This is the will of my Father who sent me: that everyone who sees the Son and believes in him may have eternal life, and I will raise him up on the last day. (Jn 6:40)

No one is able to come to me, unless the Father, who has sent me, has drawn him. And I will raise him up on the last day. (Jn 6:44)

I am the Resurrection and the Life. Whoever believes in me, even though he has died, he shall live. (Jn 11:25)

Jesus will take us to the Father

I am the Way, and the Truth, and the Life. No one comes to the Father, except through me. (Jn 14:6)

We are filled with divine truth and enlightenment

I am the light of the world. Whoever follows me does not walk in darkness, but shall have the light of life. (Jn 8:12)

I have come as a light to the world, so that all who believe in me might not remain in darkness. (Jn 12:46)

We will be able to perform signs in Jesus' name

These signs will accompany those who believe. In my name, they shall cast out demons. They will speak in new languages. They will take up serpents, and, if they drink anything deadly, it will not harm them. They shall lay their hands upon the sick, and they will be well. (Mrk 16:17-18)

Jesus will mediate and intercede for us

My little children, this I write to you, so that you may not sin. But if anyone has sinned, we have an Advocate with the Father, Jesus Christ, the Just One. (1 Jn 2:1)

There is one God, and one mediator of God and of men, the man Christ Jesus, who gave himself as a redemption for all, as a testimony in its proper time. (1 Tim 2:5-6)

We are filled with God's presence

We have seen, and we testify, that the Father has sent his Son to be the Savior of the world. Whoever has confessed that Jesus is the Son of God, God abides in him, and he in God. (1 Jn 4:14-15)

Everyone who withdraws and does not remain in the teaching of Christ, does not have God. Whoever remains in the teaching, such a one as this has both the Father and the Son. (2 Jn 1:9)

Behold, I am with you always, even to the end of the age. (Matt 28:20)

We will be delivered from Satan and his influence
Whoever commits sin is of the devil. For the devil sins from the beginning. For this reason, the Son of God appeared, so that he might destroy the works of the devil. (1 Jn 3:8)

Because children share flesh and blood, he himself also, in like manner, has shared in the same human nature, so that through death, he might destroy him who held the dominion of death, that is, the devil, and so that he might free those who, through the fear of death, had been condemned to be held in slavery throughout their entire life. (Heb 2:14-15)

Freedom from Satan's oppression
Jesus of Nazareth, whom God anointed with the Holy Spirit and with power, traveled around doing good and healing all those oppressed by the devil. For God was with him. (Acts 10:38)

We are healed of our sicknesses
The eyes of the blind will be opened, and the ears of the deaf will be cleared. Then the disabled will leap like a dear, and the tongue of the mute will be untied. For the waters have burst forth in the wilderness, and streams in the desert. (Is 35:5-6)

I have seen their ways, and I will heal them: I will lead them also, and restore comforts unto them and to their mourners the fruit of the lips; Peace, peace to them that are far off, and to them that are near, says the Lord; and I will heal them. (Is 57:18-19)

Jesus traveled throughout all of Galilee, teaching in their synagogues, and preaching the Gospel of the kingdom, and healing every sickness and every infirmity among the people. (Matt 4:23)

Through faith in his name has made this man strong, whom you see and know: and the faith which is through Jesus has given him this perfect health in the presence of you all. (Acts 3:16)

We are set free from demons and evil spirits
He has sent me to bring good news to the meek, so as to heal the contrite of heart, to proclaim liberty to captives and release to the confined, and so to proclaim the acceptable year of the Lord and the day of vindication of our God: to console all who are mourning. (Is 61:1-2)

He will cast down violently, on this mountain, the face of the chains, with which all peoples had been bound, and the net, with which all nations had been covered. He will violently cast down death forever. And the Lord God will take away the tears from every face, and he will take away the disgrace of his people from the entire earth. (Is 25:7-8)

We receive healing of emotions
I myself will be the shepherd of my sheep, and I will make them lie down, says the Lord God. (Eze 34:15)

I will seek what had been lost. And I will lead back again what had been cast aside. And I will bind up what had been broken. And I will strengthen what had been infirm. (Eze 34:16)

We receive joy (Fruits of the Holy Spirit)
Therefore, you also, indeed, have sorrow now. But I will see you again, and your heart shall rejoice. And no one will take away your joy from you. (Jn 16:22)

I will rejoice greatly in the Lord, and my soul will exult in my God. For he has clothed me with the vestments of salvation, and he has wrapped me in the clothing of justice, like a groom arrayed with a crown, and like a bride adorned with her jewels. (Is 61:10)

We will produce the fruits of the Holy Spirit
I am the vine; you are the branches. Whoever abides in me, and I in him, bears much fruit. For without me, you can do nothing. (Jn 15:5)

We become righteous
God made him who did not know sin to be sin for us, so that we might become the righteousness of God in him. (2 Cor 5:21)

Now, apart from the law, the righteousness of God, to which the law and the prophets have testified, has been made manifest. And the righteousness of God, through the faith of Jesus Christ, is in all those and over all those who believe in him. (Rom 3:22)

Various blessings
Blessed are those who have not seen and yet have believed. (Jn 20:29)

Joy

God's promise of joy
May the God of hope fill you with every joy and with peace in believing, so that you may abound in hope and in the virtue of the Holy Spirit. (Rom 15:13)

This is the day that the Lord has made. Let us rejoice and be glad in it. (Ps 118:24)

I will rejoice greatly in the Lord, and my soul will exult in my God. For he has clothed me with the vestments of salvation, and he has wrapped me in the clothing of justice, like a groom arrayed with a crown, and like a bride adorned with her jewels. (Is 61:10)

Rejoice in the Lord and exult, you just ones, and shout for joy, all you upright of heart. (Ps 32:11)

Word of Joy to claim during financial crisis
Though the fig tree will not flower, and there will be no bud on the vines. Though the labor of the olive tree will be misleading, and the farmland will produce no food. Though the sheep will be cut off from the sheepfold, and there will be no herd at the manger. But I will rejoice in the Lord; and I will exult in the God of my salvation. (Hab 3:17-18)

Judges and Attorneys

God's advice for Judges and attorneys
You shall appoint judges and magistrates at all your gates, which the Lord your God will give to you, throughout each of your tribes, so that they may judge the people with a just judgment, and not so as to show favoritism to either side. You shall not accept a person's reputation, nor gifts. For gifts blind the eyes of the wise and alter the words of the just. (Deut 16:18-20)

Judgmental Thoughts

Judging others blocks blessings
Do not judge, so that you may not be judged. For with whatever judgment you judge, so shall you be judged; and with whatever measure you measure out, so shall it be measured back to you. (Matt 7:1-2)

Therefore you have no excuse, whoever you are, when you judge others; for in passing judgment on another you condemn yourself, because you, the judge, are doing the very same things. (Rom 2:1)

But if you judge the law, you are not a doer of the law, but a judge. There is one lawgiver and one judge. He is able to destroy, and he is able to set free. (Jas 4:11-12)

K

Kindness

Blessings of being kind to others
Being kind to others heals our emotions
A kind man benefits his own soul. But whoever is cruel harms himself. (Pro 11:17)

Being kind to others brings life and honor
Whoever follows justice and kindness shall discover life and honor. (Pro 21:21)

Kingdom of God

What are the blessings we receive when we seek God's kingdom?
Our earthly needs will be met
Seek first the kingdom of God and his justice, and all these things shall be added to you as well. (Matt 6:33)

L

Laziness

How can laziness block or rob our blessings?

The intentions of the robust continually bring forth abundance. But all the lazy are continually in need. (Pro 21:5)

He who gathers the harvest is prudent. But he who snores in warm weather is a son of confusion. (Pro 10:5)

How long will you slumber, you lazy one? When will you rise up from your sleep? You will sleep a little, you will slumber a little, you will fold your hands a little to sleep, and then destitution will meet with you, like a traveler, and poverty, like an armed man. (Pro 6:9-10)

Whoever works his land shall be satisfied with bread. But whoever continually pursues leisure is most foolish. (Pro 12:11)

The slothful man does not roast that which he took in hunting: but the substance of a diligent man is precious. (Pro 12:27)

Leaders (Politicians, civil authorities)

Prayer of leaders

If, therefore, I have found favor in your sight, show your face to me, so that I may know you and may find grace before your eyes. Look favorably on your people, this nation. (Exo 33:13)

If I have found grace in your sight, O Lord, I beg you to walk with us, for the people are stiff-necked, and take away our iniquities and our sin, and so take us as your inheritance. (Exo 34:9)

Give to your servant an understanding heart, so that he may be able to govern your people, and to discern between good and evil. For who will be able to govern this people, your people, who are so many? (1 Kgs 3:9)

Give to me wisdom and understanding, so that I may enter and depart before your people. For who is able worthily to judge this, your people, who are so great?" (2 Chron 1:10)

God's promise for leaders
No one will be able to resist you during all the days of your life. Just as I was with Moses, so will I be with you. I will not leave you, nor will I forsake you. Be strengthened and be steadfast. (Josh 1:5-6)

The Lord will judge the parts of the earth, and he will give dominion to his king, and he will lift up the power of his anointed. (1 Sam 2:10)

Blessing prayer over leaders
May the Lord give you prudence and understanding, so that you may be able to rule and to guard the law of the Lord your God. For then you will be able to prosper, if you keep the commandments and judgments that the Lord instructed. Be strong and of good courage. You should not fear, and you should not dread. (1 Chron 22:12-13)

Lawsuits

God's promise for those who are faced with a lawsuit
No weapon which has been formed to use against you will succeed. And every tongue that shall rise against you in judgment, you shall resist. (Is 54:17)

Give praise, Shout joyfully. Rejoice and exult with all your heart. The Lord has taken away the judgments against you; he has turned aside your enemies. The king of Israel, the Lord, is in your midst; you shall no longer fear evil. (Zeph 3:14-15)

Loneliness

Prayer for overcoming loneliness
Look upon me and have mercy on me; for I am lonely and afflicted. The troubles of my heart have been multiplied. bring me out of my distress. (Ps 25:16-17)

God's promise for those who feel lonely
Behold, I have engraved you on my hands. Your walls are always before my eyes. (Is 49:16)

Behold, I am with you always, even to the end of age. (Matt 28:20)

I will not abandon you, and I will not neglect you. (Heb 13:5)

Lord's Day

What are the blessings we receive when we honor the Lord's day by attending Mass?
The Lord's day is a day of rest, refreshment, renewal, revival, and retreat
For six days, you shall work. On the seventh day, you shall cease, so that your ox and your donkey may rest, and so that the newcomer and the child of your handmaid may be refreshed. (Exo 23:12)

We will be materially blessed when we observe the Lord's day
How the Lord has given you the Sabbath, and, because of this, on the sixth day he distributes to you a double portion. Let each one remain with his own, and let no one go forth from his place on the seventh day. And the people rested on the seventh day. (Exo 16:29-30)

We will be spiritually blessed when we observe the Lord's day
They will keep my Sabbaths, and they will choose the things that I will, and they will hold to my covenant. I will give them a place in my house, within my walls, and a name better than sons and daughters. I will give them an everlasting name, which will never perish. (Is 56:4-5)

We will be filled with the joy of the Lord
All who keep the Sabbath without profaning it, and who hold to my covenant. I will lead them to my holy mountain, and I will gladden them in my house of prayer. (Is 56:6-7)

Lost and Missing person

God's word to claim for lost and missing people
He sustained him in a desert land, in a place of horror and a vast wilderness. He led him around and cared for him, and he guarded him like the pupil of his eye. (Deut 32:10)

Lottery Addiction

When an inheritance is obtained hastily in the beginning, in the end it will be without a blessing. (Pro 20:21)

Love

All blessings flow in love and we can receive the blessings of God only when we are in love
I may have the gift of inspired preaching; I may have all knowledge and understand all secrets; I may have all the faith needed to move mountains—but if I have no love, I am nothing. I may give away everything I have, and even give up my body to be burned—but if I have no love, this does me no good. (1 Cor 13:2-3, GNT)

Whoever does not love, does not know God. For God is love. (1 Jn 4:8)

Love for God

What are the blessings we receive when we love God?

All things turn out for good for those who love God
We know that all things work together unto good, for those who love God, who are called in accordance with his purpose. (Rom 8:28)

God bestows us with spiritual and material gifts when we love him
The eye has not seen, and the ear has not heard, nor has it entered into the heart of man, what things God has prepared for those who love him. (1 Cor 2:9)

God protects those who love him
Those who love me, I will deliver. I will protect him because he has known my name. He will cry out to me, and I will answer him. I am with him in tribulation. I will rescue him, and I will honor him. I will fill him with length of days. And I will reveal to him my salvation. (Ps 91:14-16)

God heals and blesses those who love him
The eyes of the Lord are upon those who love him. He is a powerful Protector, a Firmament of virtue, a Shelter from the heat, and a Covering from the midday sun, a Guardian from offenses, and a Helper from falling, who exalts the soul and illuminates the eyes, and who gives health and life and blessing. (Sir 34:19-20)

We will have no desire for sin if we love God with all our heart
Those who fear the Lord will not be unbelieving toward his Word. And those who love him will keep to his way. (Sir 2:15)

Those who love God will experience his love and presence
Let us love God, for God first loved us. (1 Jn 4:19)

All who love me will do what I say. My Father will love them, and we will come and make our home with each of them. (Jn 14:23, NLT)

I love those who love me. And those who seek me diligently shall find me. (Pro 8:17)

Those who love God will have understanding of his word
Those who fear the Lord will seek the things that are well-pleasing to him. And those who love him will be filled with his law. (Sir 2:16)

Those who love God will receive an eternal reward (life)
The eye has not seen, and the ear has not heard, nor has it entered into the heart of man, what things God has prepared for those who love him. (1 Cor 2:9)

God watches over those who love him
The Lord watches over those who love him; he is their strong protection and firm support. He shelters them from the heat, shades them from the noonday sun, and keeps them from stumbling and falling. He makes them cheerful and puts a sparkle in their eyes. He blesses them with life and health. (Sir 34:16-17, GNT)

Our children (family) will be blessed when we love God
God will not abandon his mercy, nor will he corrupt or abolish his own works. And he will not perish the stock of the descendants of his elect. And he will not destroy the offspring of him who loves the Lord. (Sir 47:22)

Love for Neighbor

What are the blessings we receive when we love others (neighbor)?

Unconditional love for neighbor helps us to overcome sin

Whoever loves his brother abides in the light, and there is no cause of offense in him. But whoever hates his brother is in the darkness, and in darkness he walks, and he does not know where he is going. For the darkness has blinded his eyes. (1 Jn 2:10-11)

Before all things, have a constant mutual love among yourselves. For love covers a multitude of sins. (1 Pet 4:8)

God fills us with his presence when we love our neighbor unconditionally

Most beloved, if God has so loved us, we also ought to love one another. No one has ever seen God. But if we love one another, God abides in us, and his love is perfected in us. (1 Jn 4:11-12)

If we say that we are in the light, yet hate others, we are in the darkness to this very hour. If we love others, we live in the light, and so there is nothing in us that will cause someone else to sin. (1 Jn 2:9-10, GNT)

In this way, the children of God are made manifest, and also the children of the devil. Everyone who does not do what is right, is not of God, as also anyone who does not love his brother. (1 Jn 3:10)

We will have peace and harmony when we love others

Above all these things put on love, which is the bond of perfection. (Col 3:14)

Satan has no power over people who love their neighbor (Live in love)

We know that we have left death and come over into life; we know it because we love others. Those who do not love are still under the power of death. (1 Jn 3:14, GNT)

Be angry, but do not be willing to sin. Do not let the sun set over your anger. Provide no place for the devil. (Eph 4:26-27)

We become disciples of Jesus

I give you a new commandment: Love one another. Just as I have loved you, so also must you love one another. By this, all shall recognize that you are my disciples: if you will have love for one another. (Jn 13:34-35)

We become children of God

Love your enemies. Do good, and lend, expecting nothing in return. And then your reward will be great, and you will be children of the Most High God, for he himself is kind to the ungrateful and to the wicked. (Luk 6:35)

Love your enemies. Do good to those who hate you. And pray for those who persecute and slander you, so that you may become the children of your Father in heaven. (Matt 5:44-45)

In this way, the sons of God are made manifest, and also the sons of the devil. Everyone who does not do what is right, is not of God, as also anyone who does not love his brother. (1 Jn 3:10)

We will experience God's love

If anyone says that he loves God, but hates his brother, then he is a liar. For he who does not love his brother, whom he does see, in what way can he love God, whom he does not see? (1 Jn 4:20)

Love of neighbor and eternal life
Those who hate others are murderers, and you know that murderers do not have eternal life in them. (1 Jn 3:15, GNT)

Lust

Sexual lust is a major obstacle for God's blessings
Let us not indulge in sexual immorality, as some of them did, and so twenty three thousand fell on one day. And let us not test Christ, as some of them did, and so they perished by serpents. (1 Cor 10:8-9)

Make your way at a distance from her, and do not approach the doors of her house. Do not give your honor to foreigners, and your years to the cruel. Otherwise, outsiders may be filled with your strength, and your labors may be in a foreign house, and you may mourn in the end, when you will have consumed your flesh and your body. (Pro 5:8-11)

You should not fall into the grip of passion, like a bull, in the thoughts of your soul, lest perhaps your strength may be cast down through foolishness, which would consume your leaves, and destroy your fruit, and leave you behind like a dry tree in the desert. For evil passion will destroy the one who has it. For it gladly provides enemies to him, and it will lead him to the fate of the impious. (Sir 6:2-4)

A sound heart is the life of the flesh: but passion the rottenness of the bones. (Pro 14:30)

Immediately, he follows her, like an ox being led to the sacrifice, and like a lamb acting lasciviously, and not knowing that he is being drawn foolishly into chains, until the arrow pierces his liver. It is just as if a bird were to hurry into the snare. And he does not know that his actions endanger his own soul. (Pro 7:22-23)

Do not let your mind be pulled into her ways. And do not be deceived by her paths. For she has tossed aside many wounded, and some of those who were very strong have been slain by her. Her household is the way to Hell, reaching even to the inner places of death. (Pro 7:25-27)

Lying

Prayer For freedom from the habit of lying
Deliver me, O Lord, from lying lips, from a deceitful tongue. (Ps 120:2)

God's warning to those who lie
Whoever gathers treasures by a lying tongue is vain and heartless. And he will stumble into the snares of death. (Pro 21:6)

The bread of lies is sweet to a man. But afterwards, his mouth will be filled with pebbles. (Pro 20:17)

Two kinds of things have seemed difficult and dangerous to me: a merchant will not be easily freed from his negligence, and a shopkeeper will not be justified by the sins of his lips. (Sir 26:29)

M

Marriage

Prayer over bride before marriage

You are our sister. May you increase to thousands of thousands. And may your offspring possess the gates of their enemies. (Gen 24:60)

May he grant you to find security in the house of your husband. (Ruth 1:9)

Blessing prayer over newlyweds

Increase and multiply, and fill the earth, and subdue it. (Gen 1:28)

Blessed shall you be in the city, and blessed in the field. Blessed shall be the fruit of your womb, and the fruit of your land, and the fruit of your cattle, the droves of your herds, and the folds of your sheep. Blessed shall be your barns, and blessed your storehouses. Blessed shall you be when you come in and when you go out. (Deut 28:2-6)

Blessing prayer over daughter-in-law

We are witnesses. May the Lord make this woman, who enters into your house, be like Rachel, and Leah, who built up the house of Israel, so that she may be an example of virtue, and so that her name may be honored. (Ruth 4:11)

God's promise for those who are not finding a life partner

The virgin will rejoice with singing, the young and the old together, and I will turn their mourning into gladness, and I will console them and gladden them after their sorrow. (Jer 31:13)

God's advice for marriage partners
I give you a new commandment: Love one another. Just as I have loved you, so also must you love one another. (Jn 13:34)

Prayer when choosing a life partner
May you, O Lord, who knows the heart of everyone, reveal which one you have chosen. (Acts 1:24)

What are the blessings of marriage?
Marriage gives birth to family
Male and female, he created them. And God blessed them, and he said, "Increase and multiply." (Gen 1:27-28)

Marriage purifies and make us holy
The unbelieving husband has been sanctified through the believing wife, and the unbelieving wife has been sanctified through the believing husband. (1 Cor 7:14)

Marriage protects us from sin
Where there is no hedge, a possession will be trampled. And where there is no wife, he will mourn her absence. (Sir 36:30)

Marriage heals our emotions
And if two are sleeping, they warm one another. How can one person alone be warmed? (Eccl 4:11)

Procreation (Marriage opens door to new life)
God blessed them, and he said, "Increase and multiply, and fill the earth, and subdue it." (Gen 1:28)

Conjugal joy and pleasure
Let your spring be blessed, and rejoice with the wife of your youth: a beloved doe and most pleasing fawn. Let her breasts inebriate you at all times. Be delighted continually by her love. (Pro 5:18-19)

Marriage completes and complements us

The Lord God also said: "It is not good for the man to be alone. Let us make a helper for him similar to himself. (Gen 2:18)

He who has found a good wife has found goodness, and he shall draw contentment from the Lord. (Pro 18:22)

Masturbation

Verses to meditate for those struggling with the sin of masturbation

I say to you, that anyone who will have looked at a woman, so as to lust after her, has already committed adultery with her in his heart. And if your right eye causes you to sin, root it out and cast it away from you. For it is better for you that one of your members perish, than that your whole body be cast into Hell. And if your right hand causes you to sin, cut it off and cast it away from you. For it is better for you that one of your members perish, than that your whole body go into Hell. (Matt 5:28-30)

If your hand or your foot leads you to sin, cut it off and cast it away from you. It is better for you to enter into life disabled or lame, than to be sent into eternal fire having two hands or two feet. (Matt 18:8)

If your hand causes you to sin, cut it off: it is better for you to enter into life disabled, than having two hands to go into Hell, into the unquenchable fire. If your foot causes you to sin, chop it off: it is better for you to enter into eternal life lame, than having two feet to be cast into the Hell of unquenchable fire. (Mrk 9:43-45)

Prayer to overcome masturbation

Avert all evil desires from me. Let neither gluttony nor sexual desire take hold of me, and do not give me over to shameless passion. (Sir 23:6)

Meal (Food)

Prayer of thanksgiving before meal

It is he who remembered us in our low estate: for his steadfast love endures forever: And has redeemed us from our enemies: for his steadfast love endures forever. Who gives food to all flesh: for his steadfast love endures forever. O give thanks unto the God of heaven: for his steadfast love endures forever. (Ps 136:23-26)

Medicine

Verse to meditate before taking medicine

Indeed, neither an herb, nor a poultice, healed them, but your word, O Lord, which heals all. (Wis 16:12)

The Most High has created medicines from the earth, and a prudent man will not abhor them. Was not bitter water made sweet with wood? The benefits of these things is recognized by men, and the Most High has given this knowledge to men, so that he may be honored in his wonders. By these things, he will cure or mitigate their suffering, and the pharmacist will make soothing ointments, and he will form healing medicines, and there will be no end to his works. (Sir 38:4-8)

Memories

God's promise for those who are carrying bad memories

God will wipe away every tear from their eyes. And death shall be no more. And neither mourning, nor crying out, nor grief shall be anymore. For the first things have passed away. (Rev 21:4)

Do not call to mind the former things, nor consider the things of old. Behold, I am accomplishing new things. And now, it will spring forth. With certainty, you will know them. I will make a way in the wilderness, and rivers in the desert. (Is 43:18-19)

Ministry

God's advice for his ministers
Behold, I am sending you like sheep in the midst of wolves. Therefore, be as wise as serpents and as innocent as doves. But beware of men. For they will hand you over to councils, and they will scourge you in their synagogues. (Matt 10:16-17)

Do not choose to possess gold, nor silver, nor money in your belts, nor provisions for the journey, nor two tunics, nor shoes, nor a staff. For the laborer deserves his portion. (Matt 10:9-10)

Cure the infirm, raise the dead, cleanse lepers, cast out demons. You have received freely, so give freely. (Matt 10:8)

Prayer of God's servants
Let your face shine on your servant; save me in your unfailing love. (Ps 31:16)

O Lord, God of Abraham, and Isaac, and Israel, reveal this day that you are the God of Israel, and that I am your servant, and that I have acted, in all these things, in accord with your precept. (1 Kgs 18:36)

God's promise for those who help God's servants
Whoever, in my name, will give you a cup of water to drink, because you bear the name of Christ: Amen I say to you, he shall not lose his reward. (Mrk 9:41)

Amen, amen, I say to you, whoever receives anyone whom I send, receives me. And whoever receives me, receives him who sent me. (Jn 13:20)

Whoever receives you, receives me. And whoever receives me, receives him who sent me. Whoever receives a prophet, in the name of a prophet, shall receive the reward of a prophet. And whoever receives the just in the name of the just shall receive the reward of the just. And whoever shall give, even to one of the least of these, a cup of cold water to drink, solely in the name of a disciple: Amen I say to you, he shall not lose his reward. (Matt 10:40-42)

Blessing prayer over someone who is going for ministry work
May the God of peace, who led back from the, our Lord Jesus Christ, the great shepherd of the sheep, with the blood of the eternal covenant, equip you with all goodness, so that you may do his will. May he accomplish in you whatever is pleasing in his sight, through Jesus Christ, to whom is glory forever and ever. Amen. (Heb 13:20-21)

What blessings do we receive for serving God?
Eternal life
Amen I say to you, There is no one who has left behind house, or brothers, or sisters, or father, or mother, or children, or land, for my sake and for the Gospel, who will not receive one hundred times as much, now in this time: houses, and brothers, and sisters, and mothers, and children, and land, with persecutions, and in the future age eternal life. (Mrk 10:29-30)

God will perform signs and wonders
They, setting out, preached everywhere, while the Lord cooperated and confirmed the message by the accompanying signs. (Mrk 16:20)

Our material needs will be met
Open your works to the Lord, and your intentions will be set in order. (Pro 16:3)

Money and Finances

How to be financially blessed?

Worship God (Personal prayer, family prayer, and community prayer)

You shall worship the Lord your God, so that I may bless your bread and your waters. (Exo 23:25)

The fruit of humility and fear of the Lord is riches and glory and life. (Pro 22:4)

Obey the commandments

If you will walk in my precepts, and observe my commandments, and accomplish them, I will give to you rain in its time, and the ground shall bring forth its seedlings, and the trees shall be filled again with fruit. The threshing of the harvest shall last until the vintage, and the vintage shall overtake the sowing. And you shall eat your bread to fullness, and you shall live in your land without fear. (Lev 26:3-5)

He clung to the Lord, and he did not withdraw from his footsteps, and he carried out his commandments, which the Lord had instructed to Moses. Therefore, the Lord was also with him. wherever he went, he prospered (2 Kgs 18:6-7)

So then, if you obey my commandments, which I am instructing to you this day, so that you love the Lord your God, and serve him with your whole heart and your whole soul, he will give to your land the early rain and the late rain, so that you may gather your grain, and your wine, and your oil, and your hay from the fields in order to feed your cattle, and so that you yourselves may eat and be satisfied. (Deut 11:13-15)

Observe the charge of the Lord your God, so that you walk in his ways, so that you keep his statutes, and his precepts, and ordinances, just as it is written in the law of Moses. So that may you prosper in everything that you do and wherever you turn. (1 Kgs 2:3)

Give God first place in your life
Seek first the kingdom of God and his justice, and all these things shall be added to you as well. (Matt 6:33)

Serve God with your resources and talents
Open your works to the Lord, and your intentions will be set in order. (Pro 16:3)

Read and meditate on God's Word
His will is with the law of the Lord, and he will meditate on his law, day and night. And he will be like a tree that has been planted beside running waters, which will provide its fruit in its time, and its leaf will not fall away, and all things whatsoever that he does will prosper. (Ps 1:2-3)

Forgive all your enemies
Finally, may you all be of one mind: compassionate, loving brotherhood, merciful, meek, humble, not repaying evil with evil, nor slander with slander, but, to the contrary, repaying with blessings. For to this you have been called, so that you may possess the inheritance of a blessing. (1 Pet 3:8-9)

Avoid and Flee from sin
Who has had the power to transgress, but did not transgress and to do evil and did not do it? His prosperity will be established. (Sir 31:10-11)

Prayer of material contentment

Two things I have asked of you; do not deny them to me before I die. Remove, far from me, vanity and lying words. Give me neither begging, nor wealth. Apportion to me only the necessities of my life, lest perhaps, being filled, I might be enticed into denial, and say: 'Who is the Lord?' Or, being compelled by destitution, I might steal, and then perjure myself in the name of my God. (Pro 30:7-9)

Prayer for freedom from financial debt
From the depths, I have cried out to you, O Lord. O Lord, hear my voice. Let your ears be attentive to the voice of my supplication. (Ps 130:1-2)

God's promise for those who do not have savings
My God shall supply all your needs according to his riches in glory by Christ Jesus. (Phil 4:19)

God's advice for those who are not able to save
You have looked for more, and behold, it became less, and you brought it home, and I blew it away. What is the cause of this, says the Lord of hosts? It is because my house is desolate, yet you have hurried, each one to his own house. Because of this, the heavens over you have been prohibited from giving dew, and the earth has been prohibited from giving her sprouts. (Hag 1:9-10)

God's promise for financial restoration
I will repay you for the years which the locust, and the beetle, and the mildew, and the caterpillar consumed: my great strength which I sent upon you. And you will eat with enjoyment, and you will be satisfied, and you will praise the name of the Lord your God, who has worked miracles with you, and my people will not be confounded forever. And you will know that I am in the midst of Israel, and I am the Lord your God, and there is no other, and my people will not be confounded forever. (Joel 2:25-27)

God is able to make every blessing abound in you, so that, always having what you need in all things, you may abound unto every good work. (2 Cor 9:8)

Remember that it is the Lord your God who gives you the power to become rich. He does this because he is still faithful today to the covenant that he made with your ancestors. (Deut 8:18, GNT)

I will rebuke for your sakes the devourer, and he will not corrupt the fruit of your land. Neither will the vine in the field be barren, says the Lord of hosts. (Mal 3:11)

The Lord their God will be mindful of them and restore their fortunes. (Zeph 2:7, NRSVCE)

In that time, when I will bring you home, and in the time when I will gather for you. For I will make you into renown and into praise, among all the peoples of the earth, when I will restore your fortunes before your very eyes, says the Lord. (Zeph 3:20)

The Lord has sworn with his right hand and with the arm of his strength: "Certainly, I will no longer permit your grain to be the food of your enemies. And foreigners will not drink your wine, for which you have labored. (Is 62:8-9)

Prayer for financial blessings

May the Lord, the God of your fathers, add to this number many thousands more, and may he bless you, just as he has said. (Deut 1:11)

Oh that you would bless me, and will broaden my borders, and your hand will be with me, and you will keep me from hurt and harm. (1 Chron 4:10)

God's warning for those who love money

No one is able to serve two masters. For either he will have hatred for the one, and love the other, or he will persevere with the one, and despise the other. You cannot serve God and wealth. (Matt 6:24)

Do not choose to store up for yourselves treasures on earth: where rust and moth consume, and where thieves break in and steal. Instead, store up for yourselves treasures in heaven: where neither rust nor moth consumes, and where thieves do not break in and steal. For where your treasure is, there also is your heart. (Matt 6:19-21)

Morning Prayer

What are the blessings we receive when we pray in the morning?

A person who begins the day with God will be filled with godly wisdom

Wisdom is radiant and unfading, and she is easily discerned by those who love her, and is found by those who seek her. She hastens to make herself known to those who desire her. One who rises early to seek her will have no difficulty, for she will be found sitting at the gate. (Wis 6:12-13)

Morning prayer and spiritual gifts

At first light, he will offer his heart with watchfulness to the Lord who made him, and he will pray in the sight of the Most High. He will open his mouth in prayer, and he will ask pardon for his offenses. For if the great Lord is willing, he will fill him with the Spirit of understanding. (Sir 39:5-6)

He rises in the morning, he rises to my ear in the morning, so that I may heed him like a teacher. (Is 50:4)

Make me hear your steadfast love in the morning. For I have hoped in you. Make known to me the way that I should walk. For I have lifted up my soul to you. (Ps 143:8)

Psalm 23 (A Psalm to begin the day)

The Lord is my shepherd; I shall not want.

He makes me to lie down in green pastures:

he leads me beside the still waters.

He restores my soul: he leads me in the paths of righteousness for his name's sake.

Even though I walk through the valley of the shadow of death, I will fear no evil:

for you are with me; Your rod and your staff they comfort me.

You prepare a table before me in the presence of my enemies:

You anoint my head with oil; my cup runs over.

Surely goodness and mercy shall follow me all the days of my life: and I will dwell in the house of the Lord forever.

Mocking (Mocking others)

Whoever mocks the poor rebukes his Maker. And whoever rejoices in the ruin of another will not go unpunished. (Pro 17:5)

Mother Mary

What are the blessings we receive when we honor our blessed Mother?

She is blessed and she will bring blessings with her when we invite her into our homes

Upon entering, the Angel said to her: "Hail, full of grace. The Lord is with you. Blessed are you among women." (Luk 1:28)

Behold, from this time, all generations shall call me blessed. (Luk 1:48)

She is a favored one of God and God will grant the petitions that we make through her
The Angel said to her: "Do not be afraid, Mary, for you have found favor with God. (Luk 1:30)

Mother Mary will help us (and our families) experience the power of the Holy Spirit
The Angel said to her: "The Holy Spirit will come over you, and the power of the Most High will overshadow you." (Luk 1:35)

When Elizabeth heard the greeting of Mary, the baby leaped in her womb; and Elizabeth was filled with the Holy Spirit (Luk 1:41, RSVCE)

Mother Mary will shower her motherly love which can heal many inner wounds
When Jesus had seen his mother and the disciple whom he loved standing near, he said to his mother, "Woman, behold your son." Next, he said to the disciple, "Behold your mother." And from that hour, the disciple accepted her as his own. (Jn 19:26-27)

Jesus does not refuse his mother therefore prayers offered to Mary are granted by God
He descended with them and went to Nazareth. And he was obedient to them. And his mother treasured all these words in her heart. (Luk 2:51)

Mother Mary will help us in our battle against Satan and his army
The dragon was angry at the woman. And so he went away to do battle with the remainder of her offspring, those who keep the commandments of God and who hold to the testimony of Jesus Christ. (Rev 12:17)

I will put enmities between you and the woman, between your offspring and her offspring. he will strike your head, and you will strike his heel. (Gen 3:15)

Mother Mary will intercede for us
On the third day, a wedding was held in Cana of Galilee, and the mother of Jesus was there. Now Jesus was also invited to the wedding, with his disciples. When the wine had given out, Jesus' mother said to him, "They are out of wine." (Jn 2:3, GNT)

Murder

God's warning against those who have committed murder
Envy, murder, inebriation, carousing, and similar things. About these things, I continue to preach to you, as I have preached to you: that those who act in this way shall not obtain the kingdom of God. (Gal 5:21)

Music, Songs, Singing Hymns to God

What are the blessings we receive when we sing hymns and praises to God?

Singing praises brings us into the presence of God
Worship the Lord joyfully, all the earth. Serve the Lord with rejoicing. Enter into his presence with singing. (Ps 100:2)

When they all sounded out together, with trumpets, and voice, and cymbals, and pipes, and with various kinds of musical instruments, lifting their voice on high, the sound was heard from far away, so that when they had begun to praise the Lord, and to say, "praise to the Lord, for he is good; for his steadfast love is eternal," the house of God was filled with a cloud. (2 Chron 5:13)

We offer praise to God by singing hymns
Is any of you sad? Let him pray. Is any cheerful? Let him sing psalms. (Jas 5:13)

The singers of Psalms raised their voices, and a full sweet sound increased in the great house. (Sir 50:18)

We offer our thanksgiving to God by singing songs
The Lord is my helper and my protector. In him, my heart has hoped and I have been helped. And my flesh has flourished again, and with my song I give thanks to him. (Ps 28:7)

I will wash my hands among the innocent, and I will surround your altar, O Lord, singing aloud a song of thanksgiving and telling all your wonders. (Ps 26:6-7)

I will sing to the Lord, who assigns good things to me. And I will sing psalms to the name of the Lord Most High. (Ps 13:6)

Then the priests and the Levites were standing in their offices, with the instruments of music for the Lord, which king David made in order to thank the Lord: "For his steadfast love is eternal." And they were playing the hymns of David with their hands. And the priests were sounding out with trumpets before them, and all of Israel was standing. (2 Chron 7:6)

Christian songs are inspired by God's Word and we meditate on God's Word each time we sing
Your statutes have been my songs, in the place of my pilgrimage. (Ps 119:54)

Godly music and hymns expel the Devil and demons
Whenever the evil spirit from the Lord assailed Saul, David took up his stringed instrument, and he struck it with his hand, and Saul was

refreshed and uplifted. For the evil spirit withdrew from him. (1 Sam 16:23)

If you go forth to war from your land, against the enemies who set out against you, you shall sound the trumpets repeatedly, and there shall be a remembrance of you before the Lord your God, so that you may be rescued from the hands of your enemies. (Num 10:9)

Singing praises to God fills us with the Holy Spirit
Be filled with the Holy Spirit, singing among yourselves in psalms and hymns and spiritual canticles, singing and making melody to the Lord in your hearts. (Eph 5:18-19)

While the musician was playing, the power of the Lord fell upon him. (2 Kgs 3:15)

Singing praises to God brings breakthrough and victory
In the middle of the night, Paul and Silas were praying and praising God. And those who were also in custody were listening to them. Yet truly, there was a sudden earthquake, so great that the foundations of the prison were moved. And immediately all the doors were opened, and the bindings of everyone were released. (Acts 16:25-26)

If you go forth to war from your land, against the enemies who set out against you, you shall sound the trumpets repeatedly, and there shall be a remembrance of you before the Lord your God, so that you may be rescued from the hands of your enemies. (Num 10:9)

He appointed the singing men of the Lord, so that they would praise him by their companies, and so that they would go before the army. And when they had begun to sing praises, the Lord turned their ambushes upon themselves, that is, those of the sons of Ammon, and of Moab, and of mount Seir, who had gone forth so that they might fight against Judah. And they were struck down. (2 Chron 20:21-22)

Singing to God as a community is powerful and effective (It is biblical)

O come, let us sing unto the Lord: let us make a joyful noise to the rock of our salvation. Let us come before his presence with thanksgiving, and make a joyful noise unto him with psalms. (Ps 95:1-2)

We join with the Heavenly beings when we sing hymns to God

I heard a voice from heaven, like the voice of many waters, and like the voice of a great thunder. And the voice that I heard was like that of singers, while playing on their stringed instruments. And they were singing what seemed like a new canticle before the throne and before the four living creatures and the elders. (Rev 14:2-3)

Prayer before leading worship

My heart is steadfast, O God, my heart is steadfast. I will sing, and I will make melody. Rise up, my soul. Rise up, psaltery and harp. I will arise in early morning. I will give thanks to you, O Lord, among the peoples. I will give praises to you among the nations. (Ps 57:7-10)

N

Name of Jesus

What are the blessings we receive by praying in Jesus' name?

We attain Deliverance in Jesus' name

John Said to him, "Teacher, we saw someone casting out demons in your name; he does not follow us, and so we stop him." But Jesus said: "Do not stop him. For there is no one who can act with power in my name and soon speak evil about me. (Mrk 9:38-39)

Now these signs will accompany those who believe. In my name, they shall cast out demons. They will speak in new languages. They will take up serpents, and, if they drink anything deadly, it will not harm them. They shall lay their hands upon the sick, and they will be well. (Mrk 16:17-18)

Our prayers are answered in Jesus' name

Whatever you shall ask the Father in my name, that I will do, so that the Father may be glorified in the Son. If you shall ask anything of me in my name, that I will do. (Jn 14:13-14)

You have not chosen me, but I have chosen you. And I have appointed you, so that you may go forth and bear fruit, and so that your fruit may last. Then whatever you have asked of the Father in my name, he shall give to you. (Jn 15:16)

Amen, amen, I say to you, if you ask the Father for anything in my name, he will give it to you. Until now, you have not requested anything in my name. Ask, and you shall receive, so that your joy may be full. (Jn 16:23-24)

Sicknesses are Healed in Jesus' name
Peter said: "Silver and gold is not mine. But what I have, I give to you. In the name of Jesus Christ the Nazarene, rise up and walk." (Acts 3:6)

Let it be known to all of you and to all of the people of Israel, that in the name of our Lord Jesus Christ the Nazarene, whom you crucified, whom God has raised from the dead, by him, this man stands before you, healthy. (Acts 4:10)

Signs and wonders are performed in Jesus' name
And now, O Lord, look upon their threats, and grant to your servants that they may speak your word with all confidence, by extending your hand in cures and signs and miracles, to be done through the name of your holy Son, Jesus. (Acts 4:29-30)

Sins are forgiven in the name of Jesus
To him all the Prophets offer testimony that through his name all who believe in him receive forgiveness of sins. (Acts 10:43)

Natural Calamities

Prayer during thunderstorm, monsoon, hurricane, etc.,.
Send forth your hand from on high: rescue me, and free me from the mighty waters. (Ps 144:7)

Be merciful to me, O God, be merciful to me. For my soul trusts in you. And I will hope in the shadow of your wings, until the storms passes away. (Ps 57:1)

Prayer during flooding
Save me, O God; for the waters have come up to my neck. I sink in deep mire, where there is no standing: I am come into deep waters, where the floods overflow me. (Ps 69:1-2)

Rescue me from the waterflood, so that I may not become trapped. let not the pit shut her mouth upon me. (Ps 69:15)

God' promise for people trapped in fire
When you pass through the waters, I will be with you; and through the rivers, they shall not overflow you: when thou walk through the fire, you shalt not be burned; neither shall the flame kindle upon you. (Is 43:2)

God's promise for people trapped in flooding
The Lord is good, and a comforter in the day of tribulation, and he knows those who hope in him. He protects those who take refuge in him, even in a rushing flood. (Nah 1:7-8)

The Lord sits upon the flood. And the Lord will sit as King in eternity. The Lord will give strength to his people. The Lord will bless his people in peace. (Ps 29:10-11)

Famine
The Lord shall guide you continually, and satisfy your need in drought, and make strong your bones: and you shall be like a watered garden, and like a spring of water, whose waters fail not. (Is 58:11)

Behold, the eyes of the Lord are on those who fear him and on those who hope in his mercy, so as to rescue their souls from death and to feed them during famine. (Ps 33:18-19)

I will save you from all your filth. And I will call for grain, and I will multiply it, and I will not impose a famine upon you. And I will multiply the fruit of the tree and the produce of the field, so that you may no longer bear the disgrace of famine among the nations. (Eze 36:29-30)

The Lord of hosts will cause all the peoples on this mountain to feast on fatness, to feast on wine, a fatness full of marrow, a purified wine. (Is 25:6)

Drought

I will make them a blessing all around my hill. And I will send the rain in due time; there will be showers of blessing. (Eze 34:26)

Rain in abundance, O God, you showered abroad; you restored your heritage when it languished; your flock found a dwelling in it; in your goodness, O God, you provided for the needy. (Ps 68:9-10, NRSVCE)

The Lord will open his excellent treasury, the heavens, so that it may distribute rain in due time. (Deut 28:12)

Hear them from heaven, and forgive the sins of your servants and of your people. And reveal to them the good way, along which they should walk, and grant rain upon your land, which you have given to your people as a possession. (1 Kgs 8:36)

The jar of flour will not fail, nor the bottle of oil be diminished, until the day when the Lord will grant rain upon the face of the earth. (1 Kgs 17:14)

Fire (Wild fire, Forest fire)

To you, O Lord, I will cry out, because fire has devoured the beauty of the wilderness, and the flame has burned all the trees of the countryside. Yes, and even the beasts of the field cry out to you, like the dry ground thirsting for rain, because the fountains of waters have dried up, and fire has devoured the beauty of the wilderness. (Joel 1:19-20)

Tsunami

I have placed the shore as a limit for the sea, as an everlasting precept that it will not pass. And its waves will crash, but they will not prevail; and its waves will swell, but they will not go across. (Jer 5:22)

Prayer to make when everything is lost to fire

The house of our sanctification and of our glory, where our ancestors praised you, has been completely consumed by fire, and all our admirable things have been turned into ruins. Should you restrain yourself, O Lord, concerning these things? Should you remain silent, and afflict us vehemently? (Is 64:11-12)

God's promise for those who are displaced because of natural calamities

I will gather all of you, O Jacob. I will lead together as one, the survivors of Israel. I will set them together like a flock in the fold, like a sheep in the midst of the sheep pen. (Mic 2:12)

God's promise for the world faced with pandemic (Covid, etc.)

Our God is our refuge and strength, a helper in the tribulations that have greatly overwhelmed us. Because of this, we will not be afraid when the earth will be turbulent and the mountains will be transferred into the heart of the sea. (Ps 46:1-2)

He will cast down violently, the face of the chains, with which all peoples had been bound, and the net, with which all nations had been covered. He will violently cast down death forever. And the Lord God will take away the tears from every face, and he will take away the disgrace of his people from the entire earth. For the Lord has spoken it. (Is 25:7-8)

Needs (Basic Needs, Material needs)

God's promise about our needs

My God will fully satisfy all your needs, according to his riches in glory in Christ Jesus. (Phil 4:19)

The Lord your God has blessed you in every work of your hands. The Lord your God, dwelling with you, knows your journey, how you crossed through this great wilderness over forty years, and how you have been lacking in nothing. (Deut 2:7)

He who ministers seed to the sower will offer you bread to eat, and will multiply your seed, and will increase the growth of the fruits of your justice.(2 Cor 9:10)

The young lions do lack, and suffer hunger: but those who seek the Lord shall not lack any good thing. (Ps 34:10)

God is able to make every grace abound in you, so that, always having what you need in all things, you may abound unto every good work. (2 Cor 9:8)

Consider the birds of the air, how they neither sow, nor reap, nor gather into barns, and yet your heavenly Father feeds them. Are you not of much greater value than they are? (Matt 6:26)

Seek first the kingdom of God and his righteousness, and all these things shall be added to you as well. (Matt 6:33)

Therefore, do not worry, saying: 'What shall we eat, and what shall we drink, and with what shall we be clothed?' For the Gentiles seek all these things. Yet your Father knows that you need all these things. (Matt 6:31-32)

When praying, do not choose many words, as the pagans do. For they think that by their excess of words they might be heard. Therefore, do not choose to imitate them. For your Father knows what your needs may be, even before you ask him. (Matt 6:7-8)

O fear the Lord, all you saints: for those who fear him have no want. (Ps 34:9)

The one who walks in righteousness and speaks the truth, who casts out avarice with oppression and shakes all bribes from his hands, who blocks his ears so that he may not listen to blood, and closes his eyes so that he may not see evil. Such a one will live on high; the fortification of rocks will be his lofty place. His bread will be supplied and his water will be assured. (Is 33:15-16)

Nightmares (Evil dreams), Bedwetting

When you sleep, you shall not fear. When you rest, your sleep also will be sweet. (Pro 3:24)

Non-Christians

God's promise for non-Christians
Everyone who has called upon the name of the Lord shall be saved. (Rom 10:13)

O

Obedience to God

What are the Blessings we receive when we obey God?

If you will listen to the voice of the Lord your God, so as to keep and do all of his commandments, which I instruct to you this day, the Lord your God will cause you to be more exalted than all the nations which exist upon the earth. (Deut 28:1)

Listen, my son, and accept my words, so that years of life may be multiplied for you. (Pro 4:10)

Whoever obeys me will not be put to shame, and those who work with me will not sin. (Sir 24:22, NRSVCE)

If you obey God and avoid sin, he will be pleased with you and make you prosperous. (Tob 4:21, GNT)

Who will grant to them to have such a mind, so that they may fear me, and may obey all my commandments at all times, so that it may be well with them and with their sons forever? (Deut 5:29)

If you listen to his voice and do all that I say, I will be an enemy to your enemies, and I will afflict those who afflict you. (Exo 23:22)

If you are willing, and you listen to me, then you will eat the good things of the land. But if you are not willing, and you provoke me to anger, then the sword will devour you. For the mouth of the Lord has spoken. (Is 1:19-20)

Listen to my voice, and I will be your God, and you will be my people. And walk in the entire way that I have commanded you, so that it may be well with you. (Jer 7:23)

Listen to my voice, and do all that I command you, and then you will be my people and I will be your God. So shall I uphold the oath which I swore to your fathers, that I would give them a land flowing with milk and honey, just as it is this day." (Jer 11:4-5)

Occult

How can involvement with occult block our blessings?
We become unholy
Do not turn aside to astrologers, nor consult with soothsayers, so as to be polluted through them. I am the Lord your God. (Lev 19:31)

We lose the presence of God
The soul who will have turned aside to astrologers and soothsayers, and who will have fornicated with them, I will set my face against him, and I will destroy him from the midst of his people. (Lev 20:6)

Occult practices open doors to the devil
The Spirit of the Lord withdrew from Saul, and a wicked spirit from the Lord disturbed him. And the servants of Saul said to him: "Behold, an evil spirit from God disturbs you. May our lord order, and your servants, who are before you, will seek a man skillful in playing a stringed instrument, so that when the evil spirit from the Lord assails you, he may play with his hand, and you may bear it more easily." (1 Sam 16:14-16)

OCD (Obsessive compulsive disorder)

God's promise for those suffering with Obsessive compulsive thoughts

The peace of God, which surpasses all understanding, shall keep your hearts and minds through Christ Jesus. (Phil 4:7)

Word to meditate

Whatever is true, whatever is chaste, whatever is just, whatever is holy, whatever is pleasing, whatever is of good repute, if there is any virtue, if there is anything worthy of praise: think on these things. (Phil 4:8)

Take the shield of faith, with which you will be able to quench all the fiery arrows of the evil one. (Eph 5:16)

Old Age

Prayer of an elderly person

Cast me not off in the time of old age; forsake me not when my strength fails. (Ps 71:9)

Now also when I am old and with grey hairs, O God, forsake me not; until I have proclaimed your strength unto this generation, and your power to everyone that is to come. (Ps 71:18)

God's promise for the elderly

And even to your old age I am he; and even with your hairs will I carry you: I have made, and I will bear; even I will carry, and will deliver you. (Is 46:4)

Behold, God is my savior, I will trust, and I will not be afraid. For the Lord is my strength and my praise, and he has become my salvation. (Is 12:2)

Throughout all their tribulation, he was not troubled, It was no messenger or angel but his presence that saved them. With his love, and by his mercy, he has redeemed them, and he has carried them and lifted them up, throughout all the days of old. (Is 63:9)

Oppression

God's promise for those who are oppressed
The Lord is a stronghold for the oppressed, a stronghold in times of trouble. (Ps 9:9, NRSVCE)

The Lord has freed me from every evil attack, and he will accomplish salvation by his heavenly kingdom. To him be glory forever and ever. Amen. (2 Tim 4:18)

You have prevailed over the yoke of their burden, and over the rod of their shoulder, and over the scepter of their oppressor. (Is 9:4)

I will feed your oppressors their own flesh. And they will be drunk with their own blood, as with new wine. And all flesh will know that I am the Lord, who saves you, and your Redeemer, the Strong One of Jacob. (Is 49:16)

The oppressed shall speedily be released, and that he should not die and go down to the pit, nor that his bread should fail. I am the Lord your God, that divided the sea, whose waves roared: The Lord of hosts is his name. (Is 51:14-15)

Orphan

God's promise for those who are orphaned
I will not leave you orphans. I will return to you. Yet a little while and the world will not see me any longer. But you will see me. For I live, and you shall live. (Jn 14:18)

If my father and my mother forsake me, the Lord will take me up. (Ps 27:10)

The Lord preserves the strangers; he upholds the orphan and the widow. (Ps 146:9)

I was the one who taught Israel to walk. I took my people up in my arms, but they did not acknowledge that I took care of them. I drew them to me with affection and love. I picked them up and held them to my cheek; I bent down to them and fed them. (Hos 11:3-4, GNT)

Can a woman forget her infant, so as not to take pity on the child of her womb? But even if she would forget, still I shall never forget you. (Is 49:15)

God's promise for those who have lost their father
For the sake of Jacob, my servant, and Israel, my elect, I have even called you by your name. I have surnamed you, though you have not known me. (Is 45:4)

Prayer of an orphan
For you are our Father, and Abraham has not known us, and Israel has been ignorant of us. You are our Father, O Lord our Redeemer. (Is 63:16)

Over confidence

Whosoever considers himself to be standing, let him be careful not to fall. (1 Cor 10:12)

The wise man should not glory in his wisdom, and the strong man should not glory in his strength, and the rich man should not glory in his riches. But he who glories should glory in this: to know me and to know me well. For I am the Lord, who accomplishes mercy and judgment and justice upon the earth. (Jer 9:23-24)

P

Pain and affliction

Word to claim during physical pain

May you be strengthened with all the might that comes from his glorious power, and may you be prepared to endure everything with patience and longsuffering, while joyfully giving thanks to the Father, who has enabled you to partake in the inheritance of the saints in the light. (Col 1:11-12)

The blessing of the Lord causes riches. Affliction will not be a companion to them. (Pro 10:22)

O afflicted ones, convulsed by the tempest, away from any consolation! Behold, I will set your stones in order, and I will lay your foundation with sapphires, and I will make your ramparts out of jasper, and your gates out of sculpted stones, and all your borders out of desirable stones. (Is 54:11-12)

Parents

Blessing of parents over children who are leaving home for college or job

The Lord will guard you from all evil. He will guard your life. The Lord will guard your entrance and your exit, from this time and forevermore. (Ps 121:7-8)

Promise for parents of children who are addicted to drugs

Even the captives will be taken away from the strong, even what has been taken by the powerful will be saved. And truly, I will contend with those who contend with you, and I will save your children. (Is 49:25)

God's promise for parents who are faithful and obedient to God
I will multiply your offspring like the stars of heaven. And I will give to your posterity all these regions. And in your offspring all the nations of the earth will be blessed, because Abraham obeyed my voice, and kept my precepts and commandments, and observed the ceremonies and the laws. (Gen 26:4-5)

Keep his precepts and commandments, which I am teaching to you, so that it may be well with you, and with your children after you, and so that you may remain for a long time upon the land, which the Lord your God will give to you. (Deut 4:40)

I will turn their work into truth, and I will forge a perpetual covenant with them. Their descendants shall be known among the nations, and their offspring in the midst of the peoples. All who see them will recognize them: that these are the people whom the Lord has blessed. (Is 61:8-9)

God's promise for parents who love Him
God will not abandon his mercy, nor will he corrupt or abolish his own works. And he will not perish the stock of the descendants of his elect. And he will not destroy the offspring of him who loves the Lord. (Sir 47:22)

God's promise for parents whose students are struggling with their education
All your children will be taught by the Lord. And great will be the peace of your children. (Is 54:13)

Prayer of parents
Grant my child a perfect heart, so that he may keep your commandments, your decrees, and your statutes, and so that he may accomplish all things. (1 chron 29:19)

Word to claim for children's career and future
Behold: I and my children, whom the Lord has given to me are signs and portents, in Israel, from the Lord of hosts, who lives on Mount Zion. (Is 8:18)

In the Lord, all the offspring of Israel shall be justified and shall glory. (Is 45:25)

Party Culture

God's advice for those who party excessively
Do not be willing to be in the feasts of great drinkers, nor in the carousing of those who gather to feed on flesh. For those who waste time drinking, and who surrender themselves to symbols, will be consumed. And those who sleep will be clothed in rags. (Pro 23:20-21)

Now, hear these things, you who are given to pleasures and who dwell carelessly, who say in your heart: "I am, and there is no one greater than me. I will not sit as a widow, and I will not know barrenness." These two things will suddenly overwhelm you in one day: barrenness and widowhood. (Is 47:8-9)

Patience

God's advice for those who are impatient
A short-tempered man provokes conflicts. Whoever is patient calms those who are stirred up. (Pro 15:18)

Rejoice in hope; be patient in tribulation; persevere in prayer. (Rom 12:12)

I have waited patiently for the Lord, and he was attentive to me. And he heard my prayers and he led me out of the pit of misery and the miry bog.(Ps 40:1)

Peace

God's promise of peace

These things I have spoken to you, so that you may have peace in me. In the world, you will face persecutions. But take courage: I have overcome the world. (Jn 16:33)

Peace I leave for you; my Peace I give to you. Not in the way that the world gives, do I give to you. Do not let your heart be troubled, and let it not fear. (Jn 14:27)

You will keep him in perfect peace, whose mind is steadfast: because he trusts in you. (Is 26:3)

The peace of God, which exceeds all understanding, shall keep your hearts and minds through Christ Jesus. (Phil 4:7)

Let the peace of Christ lift up your hearts. For in this peace, you have been called, as one body. (Col 3:15)

Persecution

God's promise for those who are being persecuted

If the world hates you, know that it has hated me before you. If you had been of the world, the world would love you as its own. Yet truly, you are not of the world, but I have chosen you out of the world; because of this, the world hates you. (Jn 15:18-19)

Blessed are those who endure persecution for the sake of righteousness, for theirs is the kingdom of heaven. (Matt 5:10)

Blessed are you when they have slandered you, and persecuted you, and spoken all kinds of evil against you, falsely, for my sake: be glad and exult, for your reward in heaven is plentiful. For so they persecuted the prophets who were before you. (Matt 5:11-12)

Perseverance (Endurance)

What are the blessings of perseverance?
Salvation and eternal life
Many false prophets will arise, and they will lead many astray. And because iniquity has abounded, the love of many will grow cold. But whoever will have persevered until the end, the same shall be saved. (Matt 24:11-13)

Whoever conquers, I will grant to him to sit with me on my throne, just as I also have conquered and have sat down with my Father on his throne. (Rev 3:21)

Endurance produces character and hope
We also boast in our sufferings, knowing that suffering produces endurance, and endurance produces character, and character produces hope, and hope does not disappoint us. (Rom 5:3-4, NRSVCE)

Poor, Poverty

God's promise for the poor
O Jerusalem, you suffering, helpless city, with no one to comfort you, I will rebuild your foundations with precious stones. I will build your towers with rubies, your gates with stones that glow like fire, and the wall around you with jewels. (Is 54:11-12, GNT)

The poor and the needy are seeking water, but there is none. Their tongue has been dried up by thirst. I, the Lord, will heed them. I, the

God of Israel, will not abandon them. I will open rivers in the high hills, and fountains in the midst of the plains. I will turn the desert into pools of water, and the impassable land into streams of water. (Is 41:17-18)

He has noticed the prayer of the destitute, and he has not despised their petition. (Ps 102:17)

Blessed are you poor, for yours is the kingdom of God. Blessed are you who are hungry now, for you shall be satisfied. Blessed are you who are weeping now, for you shall laugh. (Luk 6:20-21)

During these forty years your clothes have not worn out, nor have your feet swollen up. Remember that the Lord your God corrects and punishes you just as parents discipline their children. So then, do as the Lord has commanded you: live according to his laws and obey him. (Deut 8:4-6, GNT)

He has satisfied the thirsty, and he has satisfied the hungry soul with good things. (Ps 107:9)

Word of Joy for those who are poor
Though the fig tree will not flower, and there will be no bud on the vines. Though the labor of the olive tree will be misleading, and the farmland will produce no food. Though the sheep will be cut off from the sheepfold, and there will be no herd at the manger. But I will rejoice in the Lord; and I will exult in the God of my salvation. (Hab 3:17-18)

Pornography

Word to meditate for those struggling with Pornography
The lamp of your body is your eye. If your eye is wholesome, your entire body will be filled with light. But if your eye has been

corrupted, your entire body will be darkened. If then the light that is in you is darkness, how great will that darkness be! (Matt 6:22)

If your eye leads you to sin, root it out and cast it away from you. It is better for you to enter into life with one eye, than to be sent into the fires of Hell having two eyes. (Matt 18:9)

If your eye causes you to sin, pluck it out: it is better for you to enter into the kingdom of God with one eye, than having two eyes to be cast into the Hell of fire, where their worm does not die, and the fire is not extinguished. (Mrk 9:47-48)

Let each one cast away the offenses of his eyes, and do not choose to defile yourselves with the idols of Egypt. I am the Lord your God. (Eze 20:7)

Why are you seduced, my son, by a strange woman, and why are you kept warm by the bosom of another? (Pro 5:20)

Prayer
Turn my eyes away, lest they see what is vain. Revive me in your way. (Ps 119:37)

Praise

What are the blessings we receive when we praise God?
Praise frees us from sinful inclinations
While they praised God's holy name, and the sanctuary resounded from early morning. The Lord took away his sins, and exalted his power forever. (Sir 47:10-11, NRSVCE)

Praise brings us into the presence of God
Enter his gates with thanksgiving, his courts with praise, and acknowledge him. Bless his name. (Ps 100:4)

Praise frees us from negativity (Negative emotions)

I will praise the name of God with a song; I will magnify him with thanksgiving. Let the oppressed see it and be glad; you who seek God, let your hearts revive. (Ps 69:30, 32, NRSVCE)

Sing praises to the Lord, you his saints, and give thanks with remembrance of his holiness. For wrath is in his indignation, and his favor is for a lifetime. Toward evening, weeping will linger, and toward morning, gladness. (Ps 30:4-5)

Praise and worship fills us with joy and lifts our spirit

On the twenty-third day of the seventh month, he dismissed the people to their dwellings, joyful and glad over the good that the Lord had done for David, and for Solomon, and for his people Israel. (2 Chron 7:10)

Praise helps us overcome fears

In God, whose Word I praise. In God, I have put my trust. I will not fear what flesh can do to me. (Ps 56:4)

Praise heals our inner wounds

Why are you sad, my soul? And why do you disquiet me? Hope in God, for I will again praise him: the salvation of my countenance. (Ps 41:5)

Praise lifts our prayers to God

I will praise your name unceasingly, and I will praise it with thanksgiving, for my prayer was heeded. And you freed me from perdition, and you rescued me from the time of iniquity. (Sir 51:11)

Praise is a demonstration of our faith (Praise releases our faith)

They were walking in the midst of the flame, praising God and blessing the Lord. Then Azariah, while standing, prayed in this manner, and opening his mouth in the midst of the fire, he said:

"Blessed are you, O Lord, the God of our fathers, and your name is praiseworthy and glorious for all ages. (Dan 3:24-26)

The Holy Spirit comes upon us when we praise God
While the musician was playing, the power of the Lord came on him. (2 Kgs 3:15)

Do not choose to be drunk with wine, for this is self-indulgence. Instead, be filled with the Holy Spirit, speaking among yourselves in psalms and hymns and spiritual canticles, singing and reciting psalms to the Lord in your hearts, giving thanks always for everything, in the name of our Lord Jesus Christ, to God the Father. (Eph 5:18-20)

Praise removes obstacles in our lives
With all the people shouting, and the trumpets blaring, after the voice and the sound increased in the ears of the multitude, the walls promptly fell to ruin. (Josh 6:1-20)

When we praise God, we receive the anointing to speak God's Word
While the musician was playing, the power of the Lord fell upon him, and he said: "Thus says the Lord: Make, in the channel of this torrent, pit after pit." (2 Kgs 3:15-16)

Praise delivers us from evil
Praising, I will call upon the Lord. And I will be saved from my enemies. (Ps 18:3)

I will call upon the Lord, who is worthy to be praised; and I will be saved from my enemies. (2 Sam 22:4)

Praise frees us from demonic oppression

I will praise the name of God with a song, and I will magnify him with praise. And it will please God more than a new calf producing horns and hoofs. Let the oppressed see and rejoice. (Ps 69:30-32)

Healings take place when God is praised

Heal me, O Lord, and I will be healed. Save me, and I will be saved. For you are my praise. (Jer 17:14)

We will be filled with divine wisdom and knowledge when we praise God

He set his eye upon their hearts, to reveal to them the greatness of his works, so that they might highly praise his holy name, and give glory to his wonders, so that they might declare the greatness of his works. In addition, he gave them knowledge and the law of life, as their inheritance. (Sir 17:7-9)

When God is praised, all those who plot evil against us will be defeated

When they had begun to sing praises, the Lord turned their ambushes upon themselves, that is, those of the sons of Ammon, and of Moab, and of mount Seir, who had gone forth so that they might fight against Judah. And they were struck down. (2 Chron 20:22-23)

God intervenes when we praise Him (miracles, wonders, healings, and blessings are released)

In the middle of the night, Paul and Silas were praying and praising God. And those who were also in custody were listening to them. Yet truly, there was a sudden earthquake, so great that the foundations of the prison were moved. And immediately all the doors were opened, and the bindings of everyone were released. (Acts 16:25-26)

Praise brings restoration

They will praise me in the land of their captivity, and will remember my name. And they will turn themselves away from their stiff back, and from their wicked deeds, for they will call to mind the way of their fathers, who sinned against me. And I will restore them to the land which I pledged to their fathers, Abraham, Isaac, and Jacob, and they will rule over it, and I will multiply them, and they will not be diminished. (Bar 2:32-34)

Praise brings comfort in times of suffering

Give praise, O heavens! And exult, O earth! Let the mountains give praise with jubilation! For the Lord has consoled his people, and he will take pity on his suffering ones. (Is 49:13)

Praise strengthens us

Then they all together praised the merciful Lord, and were strengthened in their souls, being prepared to break through not only men, but also the most ferocious beasts and walls of iron. (2 Mac 11:9)

The Magnificat- Mary's prayer of praise

My soul magnifies the Lord. And my spirit leaps for joy in God my Savior.

For he has looked with favor on the humility of his handmaid. For behold, from this time, all generations shall call me blessed.

For the mighty one has done great things for me, and holy is his name.

And his mercy is from generation to generations for those who fear him.

He has accomplished powerful deeds with his arm. He has scattered the proud in the intentions of their heart.

He has deposed the powerful from their seat, and he has exalted the humble.

He has filled the hungry with good things, and the rich he has sent away empty.

He has taken up his servant Israel, mindful of his mercy,

just as he spoke to our ancestors: to Abraham and to his offspring forever. (Luk 1:46-55)

Prayers of praise

Blessed are you, O Lord, the God of our ancestors, and your name is praiseworthy and glorious for all ages. For you are just in all the things that you have accomplished for us, and all your works are true, and your ways are right, and all your judgments are true. (Dan 3:26-27)

Blessing, and glory, and wisdom, and thanksgiving, and honor, and power, and might, be unto our God for ever and ever. Amen. (Rev 7:12)

You are worthy, O Lord, to receive glory and honor and power: for you have created all things, and by your will they existed and were created. (Rev 4:11)

Blessing, and honor, and glory, and power, be unto him that is seated upon the throne, and unto the Lamb for ever and ever. (Rev 5:13)

Blessed are you, O Lord God of Israel, our Father from eternity to eternity. Yours, O Lord, is the greatness, the power, the glory, the victory, and to you is praise. For all the things that are in heaven and on earth are yours. Yours is the kingdom, O Lord, and you are above all rulers. Riches and honor come from you. You have dominion over all things. In your hand is virtue and power. In your hand is greatness and authority over all things. Now therefore, we give thanks to you, our God, and we praise your glorious name. (1 Chron 29:10-13)

Prayer of praise for God's plan for us
O Lord, you are my God! I will exalt you, and I will praise your name. For you have accomplished wonderful things. Your plan, from of old, is faithful. (Is 25:1)

David's prayer of praise

Blessed are you, Lord God of Israel our father, for ever and ever. Yours, O Lord is the greatness, and the power, and the glory, and the victory, and the majesty: for all that is in the heaven and in the earth is yours; Yours is the kingdom, O Lord, and you are exalted as head above all. Both riches and honor come of you, and you reign over all; and in your hand is power and might; and in your hand it is to make great, and to give strength unto all. Now therefore, our God, we thank you, and praise your glorious name. (1 Chron 29:10-12)

Word for those who don't feel like praising
Glorify the Lord as much as you are able, yet still he will far exceed this. For his magnificence is beyond wonder. Bless the Lord and exalt him, as much as you are able. But he is beyond all praise. When you exalt him, use all your ability, and do not cease in this labor. For you can never comprehend him. (Sir 43:30-32)

Prayer

Closing prayer (after making any prayer)
Let the words of my mouth, and the meditation of my heart, be acceptable in your sight, O Lord, my strength, and my redeemer. (Ps 19:14)

But as for me, my prayer is to you, O Lord. At an acceptable time, O God, in the abundance of your steadfast love, answer me. (Ps 69:13)

Your power, O Lord, is not in numbers, nor is your will with the powerful, nor from the beginning have the arrogant been pleasing to you. But the pleas of the humble and the meek have always pleased you. O God of the heavens, Creator of the waters, and Lord of all creation, hear my prayer. (Judith 9:11-12)

May these my words, by which I have prayed before the Lord, be near to the Lord our God, day and night, so that he may maintain the cause of his servant and of his people, throughout each day. (1 Kgs 8:59)

Closing prayer after praying as a community
May your eyes be open to the supplication of your servant and of your people. And so may you heed them in all the things about which they will call upon you. (1 Kgs 8:52)

Prayer pleading for an answer from God
O Lord, answer me quickly. My spirit has grown faint. Do not turn your face away from me, lest I become like those who descend into the pit. (Ps 143:7)

God's promise for family and community prayer
Again I say to you, that if two of you have agreed on earth, about anything whatsoever that you have requested, it shall be done for you by my Father, who is in heaven. For wherever two or three are gathered in my name, there am I, in their midst. (Matt 18:19-20)

God's promise for praying in Jesus' name
Whatever you shall ask the Father in my name, that I will do, so that the Father may be glorified in the Son. If you shall ask anything of me in my name, I will do it. (Jn 14:13-14)

You have not chosen me, but I have chosen you. And I have appointed you, so that you may go forth and bear fruit, fruit that will last. So that whatever you have asked of the Father in my name, he shall give to you. (Jn 15:16)

Amen, amen, I say to you, if you ask the Father for anything in my name, he will give it to you. Until now, you have not asked for anything in my name. Ask, and you shall receive, so that your joy may be full. (Jn 16:23-24)

Prayer before beginning a night vigil
My soul has desired you in the night. But I will also watch for you with my spirit, in my inmost heart. (Is 26:9)

Closing prayer after making a petition
Look with favor upon the prayer of your servant, and on his supplication, O Lord my God, and so that you may hear the prayers which your servant pours out before you. (2 Chron 6:19)

God's promise when we pray according to his will
This is the boldness which we have toward God that if we ask anything according to his will, he hears us. (1 Jn 5:14)

What are the blessings of prayer?
Prayer increases faith
When he had entered into the house, his disciples questioned him privately, "Why were we unable to cast him out?" And he said to them, "This kind is able to be expelled by nothing other than prayer and fasting." (Mrk 9:27-28)

Prayer brings spiritual blessings (fruits, charisms, gifts, favors, graces, Holy Spirit)
Ask, and it shall be given to you. Seek, and you shall find. Knock, and it shall be opened to you. For everyone who asks, receives. And whoever seeks, finds. And whoever knocks, it shall be opened to him. (Luk 11:9-10)

We receive good things from God
Or what man is there among you, who, if his son were to ask him for bread, would offer him a stone; or if he were to ask him for a fish,

would offer him a snake? Therefore, if you, though you are evil, know how to give good gifts to your children, how much more will your Father, who is in heaven, give good things to those who ask him? (Matt 7:9-11)

Prayer brings material blessings
Delight in the Lord, and he will grant to you the desires of your heart. (Ps 37:4)

Prayer helps us overcome temptations
Stay awake and pray, so that you may not enter into temptation. Indeed, the spirit is willing, but the flesh is weak. (Matt 26:41)

Watch and pray, so that you may not enter into temptation. The spirit indeed is willing, but the flesh is weak. (Mrk 14:38)

Prayer brings freedom from evil and oppression
He will cry out to me, and I will answer him. I am with him in tribulation. I will rescue him, and I will honor him. (Ps 91:15)

Take courage, my children, and cry out to God for help. He will rescue you from oppression, from the power of your enemies. (Bar 4:21, GNT)

Prayer delivers us from demons and evil spirits
When he had entered into the house, his disciples questioned him privately, "Why were we unable to cast him out?" And he said to them, "This kind is able to be expelled by nothing other than prayer and fasting." (Mrk 9:27-28)

Prayer gives us revelation about God and spiritual matters
I considered, so that I might know this. It is a hardship before me, until I may enter into the Sanctuary of God, and understand it to its last part. (Ps 73:16-17)

Cry out to me and I will answer you. And I will announce to you great things, things that are certain, though you do not know them. (Jer 33:3)

Prayer releases God's healing
They will turn to him, and he will hear their prayers and heal them. (Is 19:22, GNT)

So then, confess your sins to one another and pray for one another, so that you will be healed. (Jas 5:16, GNT)

In your infirmity, you should not neglect yourself, but pray to the Lord, and he will cure you. (Sir 38:9)

Is anyone ill among you? Let him bring in the priests of the Church, and let them pray over him, anointing him with oil in the name of the Lord. (Jas 5:14)

Prayer brings forgiveness of sins
Prayer made in faith will heal the sick; the Lord will restore them to health, and the sins they have committed will be forgiven. (Jas 5:15)

Prayer strengthens us
David was greatly saddened. And the people were willing to stone him, because the soul of every man was bitter over his sons and daughters. But David strengthened himself in the Lord his God. (1 Sam 30:6)

Preachers

Preachers' health prayer
You have taught me from my youth, O God. And so I will declare your wonders continuously, even in old age and with grey hairs. Do not abandon me, O God, while I announce your arm to every future generation: your power (71:17-18)

Verse to claim before preaching

Truly I have been filled with the strength of the Spirit of the Lord, with justice and might, in order to announce to Jacob his wickedness and to Israel his sin. (Mic 3:8)

God's promise for preachers

The Lord has given me a teacher's tongue, so that I would know how to uphold with a word, one who has weakened. He rises in the morning, he rises to my ear in the morning, so that I may heed him like a teacher. (Is 50:4)

Behold, I have placed my words in your mouth. Behold, today I have appointed you over nations and over kingdoms, so that you may root up, and pull down, and destroy, and scatter, and so that you may build and plant. (Jer 1:9-10)

I will make my words in your mouth like fire and this people like wood, and it will devour them. (Jer 5:14)

I have presented you as a tester and refiner among my people. And you will test and know their way. (Jer 6:27)

Pregnancy and Labor

Prayer during labor (for a safe delivery, complicated pregnancy and labor)

Look down upon me and have mercy on me. Grant your strength to your servant, and save the child of your handmaid. (Ps 86:16)

Prayer of blessing over a pregnant woman

Blessed shall you be in the city, and blessed in the field. Blessed shall be the fruit of your womb, and the fruit of your land, and the fruit of your cattle, the droves of your herds, and the folds of your sheep. Blessed shall be your barns, and blessed your storehouses. Blessed shall you be when you come in, and blessed shall you be when you go out. (Deut 28:3-6)

The Lord will cause you to be abundant in every good thing: in the fruit of your womb, and in the fruit of your cattle, and in the fruit of your land, which the Lord swore to your ancestors that he would give to you. (Deut 28:11)

Your offspring will be like the dust of the earth. You will spread abroad to the West, and to the East, and to the North, and to the Meridian. And in you and in your offspring, all the tribes of the earth shall be blessed. (Gen 28:14)

Presence of God

God's promise of his presence with us
I will not abandon you, and I will not neglect you. (Heb 13:5)

Be strong and courageous; be not afraid, neither be dismayed: for the Lord your God is with you wherever you go. (Josh 1:9)

When you pass through the waters, I will be with you; and through the rivers, they shall not overflow you: when thou walk through the fire, you shalt not be burned; neither shall the flame kindle upon you. (Is 43:2)

The Lord will go before you. He will himself be with you. He will neither renounce nor abandon you. Do not be afraid, and do not dread. (Deut 31:8)

Even though I walk through the valley of the shadow of death, I will fear no evil: for you are with me; Your rod and your staff they comfort me. (Ps 23:4)

I will dwell in the midst of the children of Israel, and I will not forsake my people. (1 Kgs 6:13)

What are the blessings of being in God's presence?

God's presence gives us protection for our home and family
Because you have made the Lord your refuge, the Most High your dwelling place, no evil shall befall you, no scourge come near your tent. (Ps 91:9-10, NRSVCE)

When you pass through the waters, I will be with you, and the rivers will not cover you. When you walk through fire, you will not be burned, and the flames will not scorch you. (Is 43:2)

Presence of God protects us from evil and danger
You hide them in the shelter of your presence, from the plots of men. You protect them in your tabernacle, from contentious tongues. (Ps 31:20)

He who dwells in the secret place of the most High shall abide under the shadow of the Almighty, will say of the Lord, He is my refuge and my fortress: my God; in him will I trust. (Ps 91:1-2)

Presence of God and financial blessings
Stay with the Lord; never abandon him, and you will be prosperous at the end of your days. (Sir 2:3, GNT)

The Lord your God has blessed you in every work of your hands. The Lord your God, dwelling with you, knows your journey, how you crossed through this great wilderness over forty years, and how you have been lacking in nothing. (Gen 2:7)

He who takes refuge in me will inherit the earth and will possess my holy mountain. (Is 57:13)

God's presence help us fight our battles (He fights our battles)
I said to you: 'Have no dread or fear of them. The Lord God himself, who is your leader, will fight on your behalf, just as he did in Egypt in the sight of all.' (Deut 1:29-30)

We will be filled with joy in his presence
Let all those who hope in you rejoice. They will exult in eternity, and you will dwell in them. And all those who love your name will glory in you. (Ps 5:11)

You have made known to me the ways of life; there is fullness of joy in your presence. At your right hand are delights, even to the end. (Ps 16:11)

For you will give him as a blessing forever and ever. You will make him rejoice with gladness in your presence. (Ps 21:6)

How beloved is your dwelling place, O Lord of hosts! My soul longs and faints for the courts of the Lord. My heart and my flesh have exulted in the living God. (Ps 84:1-2)

Presence of God gives us strength to live our Christian life
Be bold and be strengthened. Do not be afraid, and do not dread at the sight of them. For the Lord your God himself goes with you, and he will neither forsake nor abandon you. (Deut 31:6)

The presence of God removes all fear from us
Do not be apprehensive, nor should you fear them. The Lord God himself, who is your leader, will fight on your behalf, just as he did in Egypt in the sight of all. (Deut 1:29-30)

God's presence heals our emotions
This is said by the Most High, the Sublime One, who dwells in eternity. And his name is Holy, for he dwells in the exalted and holy

place, and also with the contrite and humble spirit, to revive the spirit of the humble, and to revive the heart of the contrite. (Is 57:15)

God's presence brings healing
You will see, and your heart will be glad, and your bodies will flourish like a plant, and the hand of the Lord will be known to his servants. (Is 66:14)

Prayer for God's presence
We follow you wholeheartedly, and we fear you, and we seek your presence. Do not put us to shame, but deal with us in agreement with your patience and according to the multitude of your mercies. (Dan 3:41-42)

One thing have I asked of the Lord, that will I seek after; that I may dwell in the house of the Lord all the days of my life, to behold the beauty of the Lord, and to enquire in his temple. (Ps 27:4)

Show me your glory. (Exo 33:18)

Pride

Pride blocks and robs our blessings
He will bend down those living in the heights. He will bring low the lofty city. He will lower it, even to the ground. He will tear it down, even to the dust. The foot will tread it down: the feet of the poor, the steps of the indigent. (Is 26:5-6)

Everyone who exalts himself shall be humbled, and whoever humbles himself shall be exalted. (Luk 14:11)

God's warning to those who are proud
Every valley will be exalted, and every mountain and hill will be brought low. And the crooked will be straightened, and the uneven will become level ways. (Is 40:4)

Priests

God's promise of strength and anointing for his priests
He will stand firm and feed his flock in the strength of the Lord, according to the majesty of the name of the Lord his God. (Mic 5:4)

God's promise of provision (Providence) for this priests

You yourselves will be called the priests of the Lord. It will be said to you, "You are the ministers of our God." You will eat from the wealth of the nations, and you will glory yourself on their riches. (Is 61:5)

Prayer of a priest for his parish
Look with favor upon the prayer of your servant and upon his petitions, O Lord, my God. Listen to the cry and the prayer, which your servant prays before you this day, so that your eyes may be open over this house, night and day, over the house about which you said, 'My name shall be there,' so that you may heed the prayer that your servant is praying in this place to you. (1 Kgs 8:28-29)

Prisoners

Prisoners prayer for release
Attend to my supplication. For I have been humbled exceedingly. Free me from my persecutors, for they have been fortified against me. Lead me out of prison so that I may give thanks to your name. (Ps 142:6-7)

Procrastination

See to it that you live carefully, not like the foolish, but like the wise: making the most of the time, because the days are evil. (Eph 5:15-16)

Promises of God

God's promise about his promises

I will not leave you, until I have done that which I have promised you. (Gen 28:15)

Let us hold fast to the confession of our hope, without wavering, for he who has promised is faithful. (Heb 10:23)

Today I am entering the way of the entire earth, and you shall know with all your mind that, out of all the words that the Lord has promised to fulfill for you, not one will pass by unfulfilled. (Josh 23:14)

The promises of the Lord are pure promises, silver tested by fire, purged from the earth, refined seven times. (Ps 12:6)

As for my God, his way is undefiled. The promises of the Lord have been proved true. He is the protector of all who hope in him. (Ps 18:30)

Every word of God proves true. He is a bronze shield to those who hope in him. (Pro 30:5)

As the rain and the snow come down from heaven, and do not return there until they have watered the earth, making it bring forth and sprout, giving seed to the sower and bread to the eater, so shall my word be that goes out from my mouth; it shall not return to me empty, but it shall accomplish that which I purpose, and succeed in the thing for which I sent it. (Is 55:10-11, NRSVCE)

God is not like a man, so that he would lie, nor is he like a son of man, so that he would be changed. Therefore, having spoken, will he not act? Has he ever spoken, and not fulfilled? (Num 23:19)

Lo, today I am entering the way of the entire earth, and you shall know with all your mind that, out of all the words that the Lord has promised to fulfill for you, not one will pass by unfulfilled. (Josh 23:14)

Blessed is the Lord, who has given rest to his people Israel, in accord with all that he said. Not even one word, out of all the good things that he spoke by his servant Moses, has fallen away. (1 kgs 8:56)

The Lord God does not fulfill his word, unless he has revealed his secret to his servants the prophets. (Amos 3:7)

Heaven and earth shall pass away, but my words shall not pass away. (Matt 24:35)

Until heaven and earth pass away, not one letter, not one stroke of a letter, will pass from the law until all is accomplished. (Matt 5:18, NRSVCE)

Prophecy (Gift of prophecy)

The Lord God does not fulfill his word, unless he has revealed his secret to his servants the prophets. (Amos 3:7)

The things that were former, behold, they have come to pass. And I also declare what is new. Before these things arise, I will cause you to hear about them. (Is 42:9)

From the beginning, I announce the last things, and from the start, the things that have not yet been done, saying: My plan will stand firm, and my entire will shall be done. (Is 46:10)

From that time, I announced the former things. They went forth from my mouth, and I have caused them to be heard. I wrought these things suddenly, and they were fulfilled. (Is 48:3)

Prostitution

God's warning for those who engage in prostitution
Do you not know that your bodies are a part of Christ? So then, should I take a part of Christ and make it a part of a harlot? Let it not be so! And do you not know that whoever is joined to a prostitute becomes one body? "For the two," he said, "shall be as one flesh." (1 Cor 6:15-16)

You should not give your soul, in any way, to prostitutes, lest you destroy yourself and your inheritance. (Sir 9:6)

Protection and Help

Prayer of thanksgiving for protection and help
I will give thanks to you, O Lord, O King, and I will praise you, O God my Savior. I will give thanks to your name: for you have been a helper and protector to me. (Sir 51:1-2)

God's promise of protection
God is faithful. He will strengthen you, and he will guard you from the evil one. (2 Thes 3:3)

For you will not go out in a tumult, nor will you take flight in a hurry. For the Lord will go before you, and the God of Israel will be your rear guard. (Is 52:12)

Psalm 91 (God's promise of protection)
He who dwells in the secret place of the most High shall abide under the shadow of the Almighty, will say of the Lord, He is my refuge and my fortress: my God; in him will I trust. He shall deliver you

from the snare of the fowler, and from the deadly pestilence. He shall cover you with his feathers, and under his wings you will find refuge: his faithfulness shall be a shield and buckler. You shall not be afraid for the terror by night; nor for the arrow that flies by day; Nor for the pestilence that walks in darkness; nor for the destruction that wastes at noonday. A thousand shall fall at your side, and ten thousand at your right hand; but it shall not come near you. Only with your eyes shall you behold and see the reward of the wicked. Because you have made the Lord, your refuge, the most High, your dwelling place; No evil befall you, neither shall any plague come near your dwelling. For he shall give his angels charge over you, to keep you in all your ways. They shall bear you up in their hands, lest you dash your foot against a stone. You shall tread upon the lion and adder: the young lion and the serpent, you shall trample under feet. Those who love me, I will deliver him: I will protect him, because he knows my name. He shall call upon me, and I will answer him: I will be with him in trouble; I will deliver him, and honor him. With long life will I satisfy him, and show him my salvation.

Prayer of protection
Protect me, O Lord, because I have hoped in you. (Ps 16:1)

Keep me as the apple of the eye, hide me under the shadow of your wings. (Ps 17:8)

You are my hiding place; You preserve me from trouble; You encompass me with songs of deliverance. (Ps 32:7)

Prayer for protection from natural calamities
Be merciful to me, O God, be merciful to me. For my soul trusts in you. And I will hope in the shadow of your wings, until the storms passes away. (Ps 57:1)

Promise of protection from evil

The Lord is your keeper, the Lord is your protection, at your right hand. The sun will not burn you by day, nor the moon by night. The Lord guards you from all evil. May the Lord guard your soul. May the Lord guard your entrance and your exit, from this time forward and even forever. (Ps 121:5-8)

Q

Quick tempered (Short temper)

Do not be quickly moved to anger. For anger resides in the bosom of the foolish. (Eccl 7:9)

You know this, my most beloved brothers. So let every man be quick to listen, but slow to speak and slow to anger; for your anger does not produce God's righteousness. (Jas 1:19-20)

The senseless immediately reveals his anger. But whoever ignores insults is prudent. (Pro 12:16)

Whoever is slow to anger is governed by much prudence. But whoever has a hasty temper exalts his foolishness. (Pro 14:29)

One who is slow to anger is better than a strong one. And whoever controls his temper is better than one who assaults cities. (Pro 16:32)

Do not become like the horse and the mule, which have no understanding. Their temper must be constrained with bit and bridle, so as not to draw near to you. (Ps 32:9)

A short-tempered man provokes quarrels. And whoever is easily angered is more likely to sin. (Pro 29:22)

R

Racism

God's comforting words for those who are victims of racism
There is no distinction between Jew and Greek. For the same Lord is Lord over all, and is generous to all who call upon him. For all those who have called upon the name of the Lord shall be saved. (Rom 10:12)

Redemption

He has rescued us from the power of darkness, and he has transferred us into the kingdom of his beloved son, in whom we have redemption, the forgiveness of sins. (Col 1:13-14)

Refugees

Prayer of refugees
Save us, O Lord our God, and gather us from the nations, so that we may give thanks to your holy name and glory in your praise. (Ps 106:47)

God's promise to refugees
The Lord your God will lead you into a good land: a land of brooks and waters and fountains, in which deep rivers burst forth from its plains and mountains, a land of crops, barley, and vineyards, in which fig and pomegranate and olive trees spring up, a land of oil and honey. In that place, without any need, you shall eat your bread and enjoy an abundance of all things. (Deut 8:7-9)

Return, you exiles who now have hope; return to your place of safety. Now I tell you that I will repay you twice over with blessing for all you have suffered. (Zech 9:12, GNT)

I will bring my people back to their land. They will rebuild their ruined cities and live there; they will plant vineyards and drink the wine; they will plant gardens and eat what they grow. I will plant my people on the land I gave them, and they will not be pulled up again. (Amos 9:14-15, GNT)

I will restore them to the land which I pledged to their fathers, Abraham, Isaac, and Jacob, and they will rule over it, and I will multiply them, and they will not be diminished. (Bar 2:34)

Rejection

God will never reject us
Thus says the Lord: "If the heavens above are able to be measured, and if the foundations of the earth beneath can be examined, then I will reject all the offspring of Israel, because of all that they have done, says the Lord. (Jer 31:37)

You, O Israel, are my servant, O Jacob, whom I have chosen, the offspring of my friend Abraham. For his sake, I have taken you from the ends of the earth, and I have called you from its distant places. And I said to you: "You are my servant. I have chosen you, and I have not cast you aside." (Is 41:8-9)

Repentance

What are the blessings we receive when we repent?
Repentance brings God's forgiveness
If they repent with all their heart and soul in the land of their captivity, to which they were taken captive, and pray toward their

land, which you gave to their ancestors, the city that you have chosen, and the house that I have built for your name, then hear from heaven your dwelling place their prayer and their pleas, maintain their cause and forgive your people who have sinned against you. (2 Chron 6:38-39, NRSVCE)

The Lord your God is kind and merciful, and if you return to him, he will accept you. (2 Chron 30:9, GNT)

Therefore, repent and be converted, so that your sins may be wiped away. (Acts 3:19)

Repentance brings God's mercy on us

Let the wicked one abandon his way, and the unrighteous man his thoughts, and let him return to the Lord, and he will have mercy on him, and to our God, for he is great in forgiveness. (Is 55:7)

Repent and pray when you need a favor from God

Strangers have devoured his strength, and he did not know it. And grey hairs also have spread across him, and he is ignorant of it. And the pride of Israel will be brought low before his face, for they have not returned to the Lord their God, nor have they sought him in all of this. (Hos 7:9-10)

They have not cried out to me in their heart, but they howled on their beds. They have obsessed about wheat and wine; they have withdrawn from me. (Hos 7:14)

Your heart was penitent, and you humbled yourself in the sight of God concerning these things which have been said against this place and against the inhabitants of Jerusalem, and since, revering my face, you have torn your garments, and have wept before me: I also have heeded you, says the Lord. (2 Chron 34:27)

Repentance leads to salvation
Sorrow that is according to God accomplishes a repentance which leads unto salvation. But the sorrow that is of the world produces death. (2 Cor 7:10)

Blessed are those who wash their robes in the blood of the Lamb. So may they have a right to the tree of life; so may they enter through the gates into the City. Outside are dogs, and drug users, and homosexuals, and murderers, and those who serve idols, and all who love and do what is false. (Rev 22:14-15)

We enter the kingdom of God through repentance
From that time, Jesus began to preach, and to say: "Repent. For the kingdom of heaven has drawn near." (Matt 4:17)

Repentance brings quietness and peace to the soul
Thus says the Lord God, the Holy One of Israel: If you return and are quiet, you shall be saved. Your strength will be found in silence and in hope. (Is 30:15)

Repentance revives us
In their tribulation, they will arise early to me. Come, let us return to the Lord. For he has seized us, and he will heal us. He will strike, and he will cure us. He will revive us after two days; on the third day he will raise us up, and we will live in his sight. (Hos 6:1-3)

Repentance makes prayer effective
Your heart was terrified, and you humbled yourself before the Lord, listening to the words against this place and its inhabitants, specifically, that they would become an astonishment and a curse, and because you have torn your garments, and have wept before me: I also have heard you, says the Lord. (2 Kgs 22:19)

Repentance brings healing to our dwelling place

If my people, over whom my name has been invoked, being converted, will have petitioned me and sought my face, and will have done penance for their wicked ways, then I will heed them from heaven, and I will forgive their sins, and I will heal their land. (2 Chron 7:14)

Repentance brings an outpouring of the Holy Spirit upon us

Repent and be baptized, each one of you, in the name of Jesus Christ, for the remission of your sins. And you shall receive the gift of the Holy Spirit. (Acts 2:38)

Repentance frees us from evil (deliverance)

Then Samuel spoke to the entire house of Israel, saying: "If you would return to the Lord with your whole heart, take away strange gods from among you, the Baals and Ashtaroth, and prepare your hearts for the Lord, and serve him alone. And he will rescue you from the hand of the Philistines." (1 Sam 7:3)

Repentance brings healings

In their tribulation, they will arise early to me. Come, let us return to the Lord. For he has seized us, and he will heal us. He will strike, and he will cure us. (Hos 6:1-2)

Do not seem wise to yourself. Fear God, and withdraw from evil. Certainly, it shall be health to your flesh, and refreshment to your body. (Rev 3:7-8)

Repentance restores God's blessings

If you will return to me, and keep my precepts, and do them, even if you will have been led away to the furthest reaches of the heavens, I will gather you from there, and I will lead you back to the place that I have chosen so that my name would dwell there. (Neh 1:9)

The son said to him: 'Father, I have sinned against heaven and before you. Now I am not worthy to be called your son.' But the father said to his servants: 'Quickly! Bring out the best robe, and clothe him with it. And put a ring on his hand and shoes on his feet. And bring the fatted calf here, and kill it. And let us eat and hold a feast. For this son of mine was dead, and has revived; he was lost, and is found.' And they began to feast. (Luk 15:21-24)

Convert, each one from his wicked way, and make your intentions good. And do not choose to follow strange gods, nor shall you worship them. And then you shall live in the land which I gave to you and to your fathers. (Jer 35:15)

Sin brings death whereas repentance gives us new life

If the wicked man turns away from all his sins which he has committed, and if he keeps all my statutes, and does what is lawful and right, then he shall certainly live, and he shall not die. I will not remember all his iniquities, which he has committed; by his righteousness, which he has done, he shall live. How could it be my will that a wicked man should die, says the Lord God, and not that he should be converted from his ways and live? (Eze 18:21-23)

I will judge each one according to his ways, says the Lord God. Be converted, and do penance for all your iniquities, and then iniquity will not be your ruin. Cast all your transgressions, by which you have transgressed, away from you, and make for yourselves a new heart and a new spirit. And then why should you die, O house of Israel? For I do not desire the death of one who dies, says the Lord God. So return and live. (Eze 18:30-32)

Repentance restores the presence of God in us

Thus says the Lord of hosts, the God of Israel: Make your ways and your intentions good, and I will live with you in this place. (Jer 7:3)

If you truly amend your ways and your doings, if you exercise judgment between a man and his neighbor, if you do not act with deceit toward the new arrival, the orphan, and the widow, and if you do not pour out innocent blood in this place, and if you do not walk after strange gods, which is to your own harm, then I will live with you in this place, in the land that I gave to your fathers from the beginning and even forever. (Jer 7:5-7)

For, from the days of your ancestors, you have withdrawn from my ordinances and have not kept them. Return to me, and I will return to you, says the Lord of hosts. (Mal 3:7)

Thus says the Lord of hosts: Turn to me, says the Lord of hosts, and I will turn to you, says the Lord of hosts. (Zech 1:3)

Repentance brings God's promises to fulfillment
The Lord is not delaying his promise, as some imagine, but he does act patiently for your sake, not wanting anyone to perish, but wanting all to come to repentance. (2 Pet 3:9)

Psalm 51 (Prayer of repentance)
Have mercy on me, O God, according to your steadfast love. And, according to the multitude of your compassion, blot out my transgressions.
Wash me thoroughly from my iniquity, and cleanse me from my sin.
For I know my iniquity, and my sin is ever before me.
Against you alone have I sinned, and I have done evil before your eyes. And so, you are justified in your words, and blameless when you give judgment.
For behold, I was born in guilt, and in sinfulness did my mother conceive me.
For behold, you have loved truth in the inward parts. therefore teach me wisdom in my secret heart.

You will sprinkle me with hyssop, and I will be cleansed. You will wash me, and I will be made whiter than snow.

Let me hear gladness and rejoicing. And the bones that have been crushed will exult.

Turn your face away from my sins, and erase all my iniquities.

Create a clean heart in me, O God. And renew an upright spirit within my inmost being.

Do not cast me away from your presence; and do not take your Holy Spirit from me.

Restore to me the joy of your salvation, and confirm me with an willing spirit.

Then I will teach the unjust your ways, and the impious will be converted to you.

Deliver me from bloodshed, O God, the God of my salvation, and my tongue will extol your justice.

O Lord, you will open my lips, and my mouth will announce your praise.

For if you had desired sacrifice, I would certainly have given it, but with burnt offerings, you will not be delighted.

A crushed spirit is a sacrifice to God. A contrite and broken heart, O God, you will not spurn.

Act kindly, Lord, in your good will toward Zion, so that the walls of Jerusalem may be built up.

Then you will accept the sacrifice of justice, oblations, and burnt offerings. Then they will lay bulls upon your altar.

Prayer of repentance

Why have you allowed us to stray from your ways, O Lord? Why have you hardened our heart, so that we do not fear you? (Is 63:16)

O God, be merciful to me, a sinner. (Luk 18:13)

Restlessness

Come to me, all you who labor and have been burdened, and I will give you rest. Take my yoke upon you, and learn from me, for I am meek and humble of heart; and you shall find rest for your souls. For my yoke is easy and my burden is light. (Matt 11:28-30)

Revenge

God's advice for those who seek revenge

Whoever wishes for vengeance will find vengeance from the Lord, and he will surely be attentive to his sins. (Sir 28:1)

Do not say, "I will repay evil." Wait for the Lord, and he will free you. (Pro 20:22)

Do not seek revenge, neither should you be mindful of the injury of your fellow citizens. You shall love your friend as yourself. I am the Lord. (Lev 19:18)

See to it that no one repays evil for evil to anyone. Instead, always pursue whatever is good, with one another and with all. (1 Thes 5:15)

You have heard that it was said: 'An eye for an eye, and a tooth for a tooth.' But I say to you, do not resist one who is evil, but if anyone will have struck you on your right cheek, offer to him the other also. (Matt 5:38-39)

Do not take revenge, dearest ones. Instead, step aside from wrath. For it is written: "Vengeance is mine. I shall give retribution, says the Lord." (Rom 12:19)

Do Not repay evil with evil, nor slander with slander, but, to the contrary, repay with blessings. For to this you have been called, so that you may possess the inheritance of a blessing. (1 Pet 3:9)

Rich

God's advice for those who desire to get rich

Those who want to get rich fall into temptation and are caught in the trap of many foolish and harmful desires, which pull them down to ruin and destruction. For the love of money is a source of all kinds of evil. Some have been so eager to have it that they have wandered away from the faith and have broken their hearts with many sorrows. (1 Tim 6:9-10, GNT)

Instruct the wealthy of this age not to have a superior attitude, nor to hope in the uncertainty of riches, but in the living God, who offers us everything in abundance to enjoy. (1 Tim 6:17)

Righteousness

We will be blessed by God if we live a righteous life

The blessing of the Lord is on the head of the righteous. But iniquity covers the mouth of the impious. (Pro 10:6)

We will be rewarded by God if we live a righteous life

The Lord will reward me according to my righteousness. And he will repay me according to the cleanness of my hands. For I have kept to the ways of the Lord, and I have not acted impiously before my God. (2 Sam 22:21)

God's promise of wisdom for those who are righteous

The Lord bestows wisdom, and out of his mouth, prudence and knowledge. He will preserve the salvation of the righteous, and he will protect those who walk uprightly. (Pro 2:6-7)

The eyes of the Lord are on the righteous, and his ears are open to their cry. (Ps 34:15, NRSVCE)

Many are the afflictions of the righteous, but the Lord rescues them from them all. He keeps all their bones; not one of them will be broken. (Ps 34:19, NRSVCE)

A righteous person will be blessed in all that he does
Tell the righteous man that it is well, for he shall eat from the fruit from his own labors. (Is 3:10)

A Righteous person will be filled with true joy
The hope of the righteous shall be gladness: but the expectation of the wicked shall perish. (Pro 10:28)

God will meet the needs of a righteous person
The one who walks in righteousness and speaks the truth, who casts out avarice with oppression and shakes all bribes from his hands, who blocks his ears so that he may not listen to blood, and closes his eyes so that he may not see evil. Such a one will live on high; the fortification of rocks will be his lofty place. His bread will be supplied and his water will be assured. (Is 33:15-16)

S

Sacraments

What are the blessings of living a sacramental life?

We are saved by living a sacramental life (Baptism)

And now you also are saved, in a similar manner, by baptism, not by the testimony of sordid flesh, but by the examination of a good conscience in God, through the resurrection of Jesus Christ. (1 Pet 3:21)

Sacraments (Eucharist) nourish and strengthen us

No man has ever hated his own flesh, but instead he nourishes and cherishes it, as Christ also does to the Church. For we are a part of his body, of his flesh and of his bones. (Eph 5:29-30)

Sacraments (Confession) saves us from addictions and sinful habits

He will turn back and have mercy on us. He will put away our iniquities, and he will cast all our sins into the depths of the sea. (Mic 7:19)

Sacraments (Annointing of the sick) heal us

Is anyone ill among you? Let him bring in the priests of the Church, and let them pray over him, anointing him with oil in the name of the Lord. (Jas 5:14)

Sacraments (Holy Matrimony, Holy Orders) purifies and make us holy

The unbelieving husband has been sanctified through the believing wife, and the unbelieving wife has been sanctified through the believing husband. (1 Cor 7:14)

Sacraments (Confirmation, Holy Spirit) helps us worship Jesus

I would have you know that no one speaking in the Spirit of God utters a curse against Jesus. And no one is able to say that Jesus is Lord, except in the Holy Spirit. (1 Cor 12:3)

Sacrifice

What are the blessings we receive when we make sacrifices?

We find life

Enter through the narrow gate. For wide is the gate, and broad is the way, which leads to destruction, and many there are who enter through it. How narrow is the gate, and how straight is the way, which leads to life, and few there are who find it! (Matt 7:13-14)

We find God

If anyone is willing to come after me, let him deny himself, and take up his cross, and follow me. For whoever would save his life, will lose it. But whoever will have lost his life for my sake, shall find it. (Matt 16:24-25)

Satan

God's promise of our victory over Satan

You, my enemy, should not rejoice over me. because when I fall, I will rise up, and when I sit in darkness, The Lord is my light. (Mic 7:8)

The God of peace will quickly crush Satan under your feet. The grace of our Lord Jesus Christ be with you. (Rom 16:20)

Behold, I have given you authority to tread upon serpents and scorpions, and upon all the powers of the enemy, and nothing shall hurt you. (Luk 10:19)

Be sober and vigilant. For your adversary, the devil, is like a roaring lion, traveling around and seeking those whom he might devour. Resist him by being strong in faith. (1 Pet 5:8-9)

Now I will shatter his yoke from your back, and I will break open the bonds that bind you. (Nah 1:13)

Submit yourselves to God. Resist the Devil, and he will run away from you. Come near to God, and he will come near to you. (Jas 4:7-8, GNT)

God's promise of protection from Satan
God is faithful. He will strengthen you, and he will guard you from evil. (2 Thes 3:3)

Word of rebuke
You, my enemy, should not rejoice over me because I have fallen. I will rise up, when I sit in darkness. The Lord is my light. (Mic 7:8)

Get behind me, Satan; You are a stumbling block to me. (Matt 16:23)

Second Coming of Christ

For the grace of God our Savior has appeared to all men, instructing us to reject impiety and worldly desires, so that we may live soberly and justly and piously in this age, looking forward to the blessed hope and the advent of the glory of the great God and of our Savior Jesus Christ. (Tit 2:11-13)

They said: "Men of Galilee, why do you stand here looking up toward heaven? This Jesus, who has been taken up from you into heaven, shall return in just the same way that you have seen him going up to heaven." (Acts 1:11)

Security

God's promise of security

Trust in the Lord and do good, so you will live in the land, and so you shall enjoy security. (Ps 37:3)

Self-control

Just like a city lying in the open and without surrounding walls, so also is a man who who lacks self-control. (Pro 25:28)

Self-confidence

Blessed is the man who trusts in the Lord, for the Lord will be his confidence. And he will be like a tree planted beside waters, which sends out its roots to moist soil. And it will not fear when the heat arrives. And its leaves will be green. And in the time of drought, it will not be anxious, nor will it cease at any time to bear fruit. (Jer 17:7-8)

Though an army should encamp against me, my heart shall not fear: though war should rise against me, yet I will be confident. (Ps 27:3)

I can do all these things in him who strengthens me. (Phil 4:13)

Do not lose your confidence, which has a great reward. For it is necessary for you to be patient, so that, by doing the will of God, you may receive the promise. (Heb 10:35-36)

Self-Denial

What are the blessings of self-denial?

We will become disciples of Jesus

If anyone is willing to come after me, let him deny himself, and take up his cross, and follow me. (Matt 16:24)

We will inherit eternal life

Anyone who has left behind home, or brothers, or sisters, or father, or mother, or wife, or children, or land, for the sake of my name, shall receive one hundred times more, and shall possess eternal life. But many of those who are first shall be last, and the last shall be first. (Matt 19:29-30)

Self-esteem (Low self-esteem)

Before I formed you in the womb, I knew you. And before you went forth from the womb, I sanctified you. And I made you a prophet to the nations. (Jer 1:5)

Even the very hairs of your head have all been numbered. Therefore, do not be afraid. You are worth more than many sparrows. (Luk 12:7)

Are not two sparrows sold for one small coin? And yet not one of them will fall to the ground apart from your Father. For even the hairs of your head have all been numbered. Therefore, do not be afraid. You are worth more than many sparrows. (Matt 10:29-31)

Self exaltation

Do not appear glorious before the king, and do not stand in the place of the great. For it is better that it should be said to you, "Ascend to here," than that you should be humbled before the prince. (Pro 25:6-7)

Self-glory

If I glorify myself, my glory is nothing. It is my Father who glorifies me. (Jn 8:54)

Not to us, O Lord, not to us, but to your name give glory. Give glory to your mercy and your truth, lest the Gentiles should say, "Where is their God?" (Ps 115:1)

Selfishness

For where there is jealousy and selfish ambition, there will be disorder and every vile practice. (Jas 3:16)

Let no one seek for himself, but for others. (1 Cor 10:24)

Self-importance

I say, through the grace that has been given to me, to all who are among you: not to think of yourself more highly than you ought to think, but think unto sobriety and just as God has distributed a share of the faith to each one. (Rom 12:3)

Self-indulgence

Woe to you, scribes and Pharisees, you hypocrites! For you clean what is outside the cup and the dish, but on the inside you are full of avarice and self-indulgence. (Matt 23:25)

Self justification

He said to them: "You are the ones who justify yourselves in the sight of men. But God knows your hearts. For what is lifted up by men is an abomination in the sight of God. (Luk 16:15)

Self praise

Let another praise you, and not your own mouth: an outsider, and not your own lips. (Pro 27:2)

Self righteousness

He saved us, not by works of righteousness that we had done, but, in accord with his mercy, by the washing of regeneration and by the renovation of the Holy Spirit. (Tit 3:5)

For it is not through our righteousness that we offer requests before your face, but through the fullness of your compassion. (Dan 9:18)

Self seeking

Therefore, all things whatsoever that you wish that men would do to you, do so also to them. For this is the law and the prophets. (Matt 7:12)

Sexual Sins

Sexual sins are one of the main reasons why our blessings are blocked
Sexual sins cause inner wounds
Whoever is an adulterer, because of the emptiness of his heart, will destroy his own soul. He gathers shame and dishonor to himself, and his disgrace will not be wiped away. (Pro 6:32-33)

Sexual sins wound our body (the temple of the Holy Spirit)
Do you not know that you are the Temple of God, and that the Spirit of God lives within you? But if anyone violates the Temple of God, God will destroy him. For the Temple of God is holy, and you are that Temple. (1 Cor 3:16-17)

Sexual sins block us from entering God's Kingdom
Envy, murder, inebriation, carousing, and similar things. About these things, I continue to preach to you, as I have preached to you: that those who act in this way shall not obtain the kingdom of God. (Gal 5:21)

Sexual sins cause physical sicknesses in us
A sound heart is life for the flesh. But passion is decay for the bones. (Pro 14:30)

Sexual sins open doors to demons
Immediately, he follows her, like an ox being led to the sacrifice, and like a lamb acting lasciviously, and not knowing that he is being drawn foolishly into chains, until the arrow pierces his liver. It is just as if a bird were to hurry into the snare. And he does not know that his actions endanger his own soul. (Pro 7:22-23)

Sexual sins are serious and mortal sins
Do not let your mind be pulled into her ways. And do not be deceived by her paths. For she has tossed aside many wounded, and some of those who were very strong have been slain by her. Her household is the way to Hell, reaching even to the inner places of death. (Pro 7:25-27)

Sexual sins can affect the family line (family tree)
The children of adulterers will not reach maturity, and the offspring of a sinful bed will be banished. (Wis 3:16)

All the children born from iniquity are witnesses of wickedness against their parents when God examines them. (Wis 4:6)

Shame and embarrassment

Do not be afraid! For you will not be ashamed. Do not be discouraged, for you will not be put to disgrace. (Is 54:4)

The Lord God is my helper. Therefore, I have not been disgraced. Therefore, I have set my face like a very hard rock, and I know that I will not be put to shame. (Is 50:7)

Because their shame was double, and dishonor was proclaimed as their lot, they will possess double in their land. Everlasting joy will be for them. (Is 61:7)

Shyness

God has not given us a spirit of cowardice, but of power, and of love, and of a sound mind. (2 Tim 1:7)

Those who fear the Lord will tremble at nothing, and they will not be terrified. For he is their hope. (Sir 34:16)

Sin

How does sins block and rob our blessings?
Sin takes us away from the presence of God
Do not cast me away from your presence; and do not take your Holy Spirit from me. (Ps 51:11)

He who has acted arrogantly will not dwell in the midst of my house. He who has spoken iniquity shall not continue in my presence. (Ps 101:7)

Sin takes away the power of the Holy Spirit from us
Do not cast me away from your presence; and do not take your Holy Spirit from me. (Ps 51:11)

Sin makes us hide from God (takes away the desire to pray, read the Bible, and to go to Church)
When they had heard the voice of the Lord God taking a walk in Paradise in the afternoon breeze, Adam and his wife hid themselves from the face of the Lord God in the midst of the trees of Paradise. And the Lord God called Adam and said to him: "Where are you?" And he said, "I heard your voice in Paradise, and I was afraid, because I was naked, and so I hid myself." (Gen 3:8-10)

Sin robs our God given blessings
After he had consumed it all, a great famine occurred in that region, and he began to be in need. And he went and attached himself to one of the citizens of that region. And he sent him to his farm, in order to feed the swine. And he wanted to fill his belly with the scraps that the swine ate. But no one would give it to him. (Luk 15:14-16)

Whoever nurtures promiscuous women will lose his substance. (Pro 29:3)

They have not said in their heart: 'Let us dread the Lord our God, who gives us the timely and the late rains, in their proper time, who guards the full measure of the yearly harvest for us.' Your iniquities have turned these things away, and your sins have held back good things from you. (Jer 5:24-25)

If you obey God and avoid sin, he will be pleased with you and make you prosperous. (Tob 4:21, GNT)

Sin leads to death
The wages of sin is death. But the free gift of God is eternal life in Christ Jesus our Lord. (Rom 6:23)

When desire has conceived, it gives birth to sin. Yet truly sin, when it has been consummated, produces death. (Jas 1:15)

Therefore, just as through one man sin entered into this world, and through sin, death; so also death was transferred to all men, to all who have sinned. (Rom 5:12)

A sinner has no peace
Weapons and swords are on the way of the perverse. But he who guards his own soul withdraws far from them. (Pro 22:5)

Cain said to the Lord: "My iniquity is too great to deserve kindness. Behold, you have cast me out this day before the face of the earth, and from your face I will be hidden; and I will be a vagrant and a fugitive on the earth. Therefore, anyone who finds me will kill me." (Gen 4:13-14)

"There is no peace for the wicked," says the Lord. (Is 48:22)

Sin leads to Hell and eternal punishment
The synagogue of sinners is like stubble piled up; for the end of them both is a burning fire. The way of sinners is paved and level, and at their end is hell and darkness and punishments. (Sir 21:9-10)

Sin makes us its slave
Very truly, I tell you, everyone who commits sin is a slave to sin. The slave does not have a permanent place in the household; the son has a place there forever. (Jn 8:34-35)

Every sin has punishment built into it (e.g., smoking causes cancer)
You sent upon them a multitude of mute beasts for vengeance, so that they might know that by whatever things a man sins, by the same also is he tormented. (Wis 11:15-16)

Your sin shall overtake you. (Num 32:23)

Your own malice will punish you, and your own apostasy will rebuke you! But know and perceive this: it is an evil and bitter thing for you to forsake the Lord your God, and to be without my fear within you, says the Lord, the God of hosts. (Jer 2:19)

For the day of the Lord is near, over all nations. Just as you have done, so will it be done to you. He will turn back your retribution on your own head. (Obad 1:15)

Your ways and your thoughts have brought these things upon you. This is your own wickedness. And it is bitter, because it has touched your heart. (Jer 4:18)

Individual sins can affect the whole family (family line)
You bent your thigh to women, and you were held by the power of your body. You brought a stain upon your glory, and you profaned your seed, so as to bring wrath upon your children, and to incite your foolishness, so that you would cause the kingdom to be divided, and an obstinate kingdom to rule from Ephraim. (Sir 47:20-21)

The Lord said to Solomon: "Because you have this with you, and because you have not kept my covenant and my precepts, which I commanded to you, I will tear apart your kingdom, and I will give it to your servant. Yet truly, I will not do it in your days, for the sake of your father David. From the hand of your son, I will tear it away. (1 Kgs 11:11-12)

Why have you despised the word of the Lord, so that you did evil in my sight? You have struck down Uriah the Hittite with the sword. And you have taken his wife as a wife for yourself. And you have put him to death with the sword of the sons of Ammon. For this reason, the sword shall not withdraw from your house, even perpetually, because you have despised me, and you have taken the

wife of Uriah the Hittite, so that she may be your wife.' (2 Sam 12:9-10)

If you will not keep and do all the words of this law, which have been written in this volume, and fear his glorious and terrible name, that is, the Lord your God, then the Lord will increase your plagues, and the plagues of your offspring, plagues great and long-lasting, infirmities very grievous and continuous. (Deut 28:58-59)

Sin brings guilt in us (worldly sorrow)
For the sorrow that is according to God accomplishes a repentance which is steadfast unto salvation. But the sorrow that is of the world accomplishes death. (2 Cor 7:10)

Sin brings self-hatred
He said to them mildly, "Approach toward me." And when they had approached close by, he said: "I am Joseph, your brother, whom you sold into Egypt. Do not be distressed or angry with yourselves, and let it not seem to you to be a hardship that you sold me into these regions. For God sent me before you into Egypt for your salvation." (Gen 45:4-5)

Sin brings self-condemnation
Therefore, there is now no condemnation for those who are in Christ Jesus, who are not walking according to the flesh. (Rom 8:1)

A sinner feels unworthy of himself
Are not two sparrows sold for one small coin? And yet not one of them will fall to the ground without your Father. For even the hairs of your head have all been numbered. Therefore, do not be afraid. You are worth more than many sparrows. (Matt 10:29-31)

Sin brings shame
They were both naked: Adam, of course, and his wife. And they were not ashamed. (Gen 2:25)

251

She took from its fruit, and she ate. And she gave to her husband, who ate. And the eyes of them both were opened. And when they realized themselves to be naked, they joined together fig leaves and made coverings for themselves. (Gen 3:6-7)

A sinner feels unloved by God
God proves his love for us in that, while we were yet sinners, at the proper time, Christ died for us. (Rom 5:8)

A sinner feels abandoned and lonely
Indeed, if we sin, we are yours, knowing your greatness; and, if we do not sin, we know that we are counted with you. (Wis 15:2)

Sin closes doors of blessings (opens doors to curses)
Behold, the hand of the Lord has not been shortened, so that it cannot save, and his ear has not been blocked, so that it cannot hear. But your iniquities have made a division between you and your God, and your sins have concealed his face from you, so that he would not hear. (Is 59:1-2)

Let us dread the Lord our God, who gives us the timely and the late rains, in their proper time, who guards the full measure of the yearly harvest for us.' Your iniquities have turned these things away, and your sins have held back good things from you. (Jer 5:24-25)

He said to him: "What have you done? The voice of your brother's blood cries out to me from the land. Now, therefore, you will be cursed upon the land, which opened its mouth and received the blood of your brother at your hand. When you work it, it will not give you its fruit; a vagrant and a fugitive shall you be upon the land." (Gen 4:10-12)

Lift your eyes straight up, and see where you did not debase yourself. You were sitting in the roadways, waiting for them, like a robber in the wilderness. And you have polluted the land by your fornications and by your wickedness. For this reason, the rain showers were withheld, and there were no late season rains. (Jer 3:2-3)

Sin tries to control us and make us slaves of it (addictions)
Let not sin reign in your mortal body, such that you would obey its desires. (Rom 6:12)

If you behave well, will you not be accepted? But if you behave badly, will not sin at once be present at the door? And so its desire is for you, but you must master it. (Gen 4:7)

Jesus answered them: "Amen, amen, I say to you, that everyone who commits sin is a slave of sin." (Jn 8:34)

Do you not know to whom you are offering yourselves as servants under obedience? You are the servants of whomever you obey: whether of sin, unto death, or of obedience, unto justice. (Rom 6:16)

Hell is reserved for those who don't repent
The synagogue of sinners is like stubble piled up; for the end of them both is a burning fire. (Sir 21:10)

Sin leads to sickness
Afterwards, Jesus found him in the temple, and he said to him: "Behold, you have been healed. Do not choose to sin further, otherwise something worse may happen to you." (Jn 5:14)

Your arrows have been driven into me, and your hand has been confirmed over me. There is no health in my flesh before the face of your wrath. There is no peace for my bones before the face of my sins. For my iniquities have walked over my head, and they have been like a heavy burden weighing upon me. My sores have decayed and been corrupted before the face of my foolishness. (Ps 38:3-6)

I also will do these things to you. I will quickly visit you with destitution, and burning heat, which will waste away your eyes, and consume your lives. In vain will you sow your seed, which will be devoured by your enemies. (Lev 26:16)

For what reason shall I continue to strike you, as you increase transgressions? The entire head is feeble, and the entire heart is grieving. From the sole of the foot, even to the top of the head, there is no soundness within. Wounds and bruises and swelling sores: these are not bandaged, nor treated with medicine, nor soothed with oil. (Is 1:5-6)

A sinful person keeps adding more sins
A wicked heart will be burdened with sorrows, and a sinner will add further sins. (Sir 3:27)

Sin breeds sin
Behold, his sons arrived from the field. And hearing what had happened, they were very angry, because he had done a filthy thing in Israel and, in violating a daughter of Jacob, had perpetrated an unlawful act. (Gen 34:7)

Sin attracts evil spirits
Behold, these ones have broken the yoke all the more; they have torn apart the bonds. For this reason, a lion from the forest has struck them down, a wolf toward evening has laid waste to them, a leopard lies in wait over their cities. All who go out from there will be taken. For their transgressions have been multiplied; their rebellions have been strengthened. (Jer 5:5-6)

Sin makes holiness and eternal life harder to attain
He cast out Adam. And in front of the Paradise of enjoyment, he placed the Cherubim with a flaming sword, turning together, to guard the way to the tree of life. (Gen 3:24)

Sin wounds our relationship with God (Sin blocks our prayer life)
Your iniquities have made a division between you and your God, and your sins have concealed his face from you, so that he would not hear. (Is 59:2)

And so, when you extend your hands, I will avert my eyes from you. And when you multiply your prayers, I will not heed you. For your hands are full of blood. (Is 1:15-16)

Then they will cry to the Lord, but he will not answer them; he will hide his face from them at that time, because they have acted wickedly. (Mic 3:5, NRSVCE)

Whatever we shall request of him, we shall receive from him. For we keep his commandments, and we do the things that are pleasing in his sight. (1 Jn 3:22)

Whoever turns away his ears from listening to the law: his prayer will be detestable. (Pro 28:9)

If I have seen iniquity in my heart, the Lord would not heed me. And yet, God has heeded me and he has attended to the voice of my supplication. (Ps 66:18-19)

God's promise for those struggling to overcome sin
We know that everyone who is born of God does not sin. Instead, the one who was born of God protects him, and the evil one cannot touch him. (1 Jn 5:18)

I will place my Spirit within you so that you may walk in my precepts and keep my ordinances. (Eze 36:27)

All those who have been born of God do not commit sin. For the offspring of God abides in them, and he cannot sin, because he was born of God. (1 Jn 3:9)

He will turn back and have mercy on us. He will subdue our iniquities, and he will cast all our sins into the depths of the sea. (Mic 7:19)

God's unfailing love for a sinner

God proves his love for us in that, while we were yet sinners, at the proper time, Christ died for us. (Rom 5:8)

For a brief moment, I have forsaken you, and with great compassion, I will gather you. In a moment of indignation, I have hidden my face from you, for a little while. But with everlasting love, I have taken pity on you, said your Redeemer, the Lord. (Is 54:7-8)

Prayer of a sinner

Why have you allowed us to stray from your ways, O Lord? Why have you hardened our heart, so that we do not fear you? Return, for the sake of your servants, the tribes of your inheritance. (Is 63:17)

O Lord, though our iniquities testify against us, act Lord, for your name's sake: for our backslidings are many; we have sinned against you. (Jer 14:7)

Prayer for God's mercy when we have fallen into mortal sin

And now, O Lord, you are our Father, yet truly, we are clay. And you are our Maker, and we are all the works of your hands. Do not be so angry, O Lord, and no longer call to mind our iniquity. Behold, consider that we are all your people. (Is 64:8-9)

Sleep

God's promise for those suffering from Sleep disorder (insomnia)
I laid down and slept; I awaked; for the Lord sustained me. (Ps 3:5)

I will sleep and I will rest in peace. For you, O Lord, make me lie down in safety. (Ps 4:8)

For people with disturbed sleep
I have satiated the weary soul, and I have replenished all who are faint. Therefore I awoke, and looked; and my sleep was pleasant unto me. (Jer 31:25-26)

For people who oversleep
Laziness sends one into a deep sleep, and a dissolute soul will go hungry. (Pro 19:15)

Do not love sleep, lest deprivation oppress you. Open your eyes and be satisfied with bread. (Pro 20:13)

Those who sleep will be clothed in rags. (Pro 23:21)

For those who experience nightmares (Evil dreams)
When you sleep, you shall not fear. When you rest, your sleep also will be sweet. (Pro 3:24)

Sloth in Spiritual life (Acedia)

Spiritual sloth can block our blessings
He who had received one talent, approaching, said: 'Lord, I know that you are a hard man. You reap where you have not sown, and gather where you have not scattered. And so, being afraid, I went out and hid your talent in the earth. Behold, you have what is yours.' But his lord said to him in response: 'You evil and lazy servant! You knew that I reap where I have not sown, and gather where I have not scattered. (Matt 25:24-26)

The way of the slothful is like a hedge of thorns. The way of the just is without offense. (Pro 15:19)

Joshua said to them: "For how long will you draw back in idleness, and not enter to possess the land, which the Lord, the God of your fathers, has given to you? (Josh 18:3)

Smoking (Tobacco)

God's warning for smokers

If anyone violates the Temple of God, God will destroy him. For the Temple of God is holy, and you are that Temple. (1 Cor 3:17)

Do you not know to whom you are offering yourselves as servants under obedience? You are the servants of whomever you obey: whether of sin, unto death, or of obedience, unto justice. (Rom 6:16)

Behold, all you who kindle a fire, wrapped in flames: walk in the light of your fire and in the flames that you have kindled. This is what you shall have from my hand; You will sleep in anguish. (Is 50:11)

Soldiers (Army, war, battle)

Blessing prayer over soldiers who go to war

Blessed are you. Who is like you, the people who are saved by the Lord? He is the shield of your help and the sword of your glory. Your enemies will refuse to acknowledge you, and so you shall tread upon their necks. (Deut 33:29)

God's promise for soldiers when they go to war

The Lord God will take away, in your sight, nations that are great and very robust, and no one will be able to withstand you. One of you shall pursue a thousand men of the enemies. For the Lord your God himself will fight on your behalf, just as he promised. (Josh 23:9-10)

Blessed is the Lord, my God, who trains my hands for the battle and my fingers for the war. My mercy and my refuge, my supporter and my deliverer, my protector and him in whom I have hoped: he subdues my people under me. (Ps 144:1-2)

The men who make war against you will be like something that has been consumed. For I, the Lord your God, hold your right hand; it is I who say to you, "Do not fear, I will help you." (Is 41:12-13)

Commander's Words of encouragement for soldiers before going to war
Be Strong. And let us fight on behalf of our people and the city of our God. Then the Lord will do what is good in his own sight. (2 Sam 10:12)

Do not be afraid. Neither should you be dismayed by this multitude. For the fight is not yours, but God's. (2 Chron 20:15)

Do not be afraid. Stand firm and see the great wonders of the Lord, which he will do today. For the enemy, whom you now see, will never again be seen, forever. The Lord will fight on your behalf, and you will remain silent. (Exo 14:13-14)

Sorrow and sadness

They will approach with weeping. And I will lead them back with consolations. And I will lead them through the torrents of water, by an upright way, and they will not stumble in it. For I have become Father to Israel, and Ephraim is my firstborn. (Jer 31:9)

Now, those who have been redeemed by the Lord will return. And they will arrive in Zion, praising. And everlasting rejoicing will be upon their heads. They will take hold of gladness and rejoicing. Sorrow and sighing will flee away. (Is 51:11)

Soul

What shall it profit a man, if he gain the whole world, and suffer the loss of his soul? Or what shall a man give in exchange for his soul? (Mrk 8:36-37)

Speech

Our words can either bring a blessing or block a blessing in us
For every idle word which men will have spoken, they shall render an account in the day of judgment. For by your words shall you be justified, and by your words shall you be condemned. (Matt 12:36-37)

The evil are ensnared by the transgression of their lips, but the righteous escape from trouble. From the fruit of the mouth one is filled with good things. (Pro 12:13-14)

A peaceful tongue is a tree of life. But that which is immoderate will crush the spirit. (Pro 15:4)

Prayer for control over speech
O Lord, set a guard over my mouth and a door enclosing my lips. (Ps 141:3)

I will keep to my ways, so that I will not offend with my tongue. I posted a guard at my mouth, when a sinner took up a position against me. (Ps 39:1)

Prayer of repentance for sinful speech
"Woe to me! I am lost. For I am a man of unclean lips, and I live in the midst of a people having unclean lips." (Is 6:5)

Prayer for maturity in speech

O Lord, set a guard over my mouth and keep watch over the door enclosing my lips. (Ps 141:3)

God's promise for those who speak evil (gossip, slander, impure speech)

I will change the speech of the people to a pure speech, that they may all call upon the name of the Lord, to serve him with one accord. (Zeph 3:9)

Spiritual warfare

Armor of God Prayer

Finally, be strong in the Lord, and in the power of his might. Put on the whole armor of God, so that you may be able to stand against the wiles of the devil. For we wrestle not against flesh and blood, but against principalities, against powers, against the rulers of the darkness of this world, against spiritual wickedness in high places. Therefore take unto you the whole armor of God, so that you may be able to withstand in the evil day, and having done everything, to stand firm. Stand therefore, having your loins girded with the belt of truth, and having on the breastplate of righteousness; And for your feet put on whatever will prepare you for the proclamation of the gospel of peace; Above all, taking the shield of faith, with which you shall be able to quench all the fiery darts of the wicked. And take the helmet of salvation, and the sword of the Spirit, which is the word of God. (Eph 6:10-17)

God's promise about our battle with the spiritual forces

Little children, you are from God, and have conquered them; for the one who is in you is greater than the one who is in the world. (1 Jn 4:4, NRSVCE)

The Lord will grant that your enemies, who rise up against you, to be defeated before you. They will come against you by one way, and they will flee before you seven ways. (Deut 28:7)

No weapon that is fashioned against you shall prosper, and you shall confute every tongue that rises against you in judgment. (Is 54:17, NRSVCE)

For though we walk in the flesh, we do not battle according to the flesh. (2 Cor 10:3)

I struck them down, so that they were not able to rise; they fell under my feet. For you girded me with strength for the battle; you made my assailants sink under me. (Ps 18:38-39, NRSVCE)

Through you we push down our foes; through your name we tread down our assailants. (Ps 44:5, NRSVCE)

Though an army encamp against me, my heart shall not fear; though war rise up against me, yet I will be confident. (Ps 27:3, NRSVCE)

Let God rise up, let his enemies be scattered; let those who hate him flee before him. As smoke is driven away, so drive them away; as wax melts before the fire, let the wicked perish before God. (Ps 68:1-2, NRSVCE)

A thousand may fall at your side, ten thousand at your right hand, but it will not come near you. You will only look with your eyes and see the punishment of the wicked. (Ps 91:7-8, NRSVCE)

If God is for us, who is against us? (Rom 8:31)

You should not fear them. For the Lord your God will fight on your behalf. (Deut 3:22)

Your hand shall be lifted up over your adversaries, and all your enemies shall be cut off. (Mic 5:9, NRSVCE)

One of you shall pursue a thousand men of the enemies. For the Lord your God himself will fight on your behalf, just as he promised. (Josh 23:10)

The weapons of our battles are not merely human, but they have divine power for the destruction of strongholds: tearing down every argument and obstacle that extols itself contrary to the wisdom of God, and we take every thought captive to obey to Christ. (2 Cor 10:4-5)

The Lord God himself, who is your leader, will fight on your behalf, just as he did in Egypt in the sight of all. (Deut 1:30)

All who fight against you shall be confounded and ashamed. They will be as if they did not exist, and the men who contradict you will perish. You will seek them, and you will not find them. The men who rebel against you will be as if they did not exist. And the men who make war against you will be like something that has been consumed. For I, the Lord your God, hold your right hand; it is I who say to you, "Do not fear, I will help you (Is 41:11-13)

Who is God except the Lord? And who is a rock, except our God? God, he has girded me with strength, and he has made my way perfect: making my feet like the feet of deer, and stationing me upon my exalted places, teaching my hands to do battle, and making my arms like a bow of brass. (2 Sam 22:32-35)

Spiritual warfare prayer
Rise up, O Lord, and let your enemies be scattered, and let those who hate you flee from your face. (Num 10:35)

Sports, Sportsmen, Games

God's promise for players who want to win a game
You, who fear my name, the Sun of justice will arise, with healing in his wings. And you will go forth and leap like the calves of the herd. And you will trample the impious, while they will be ashes under the sole of your foot, on the day that I act, says the Lord of hosts. (Mal 4:2)

Word to meditate and claim
The Lord God is my strength. And he will set my feet like those of the stag. And he, the victor, will lead me beyond my high places while singing psalms. (Hab 3:19)

Who is God except the Lord? And who is a rock, except our God? God, he has girded me with strength, and he has made my way perfect: making my feet like the feet of deer, and stationing me upon my exalted places, teaching my hands to do battle, and making my arms like a bow of brass. (2 Sam 22:32-35)

Stealing

Whoever was stealing, let him now not steal, but rather let him labor, working with his hands, doing what is good, so that he may have something to distribute to those who suffer need. (Eph 4:28)

Stinginess (Miserly)

Riches are inappropriate for a covetous man and a miser, and what should an envious man do with gold? He that gathers together by wronging his own soul, gathers for others, and another will squander away his goods in rioting. He that is evil to himself, to whom will he be good? and he shall not take pleasure in his goods. (Sir 14:3-5)

Stock Market addiction

When an inheritance is obtained hastily in the beginning, in the end it will be without a blessing. (Pro 20:21)

Strength

Word to meditate to be filled with the gift of fortitude
The Lord is my strength and my praise. And he has become my salvation. (Ps 118:14)

I can do all these things in him who strengthens me. (Phil 4:13)

It is he that gives power to the weary, and strengthens them that are powerless. Youths shall faint, and labor, and young men shall fall exhausted. But they that hope in the Lord shall renew their strength, they shall take wings as eagles, they shall run and not be weary, they shall walk and not faint. (Is 40:29-31)

Stress

Come to me, all you who labor and have been burdened, and I will give you rest. Take my yoke upon you, and learn from me, for I am meek and humble of heart; and you shall find rest for your souls. For my yoke is easy and my burden is light. (Matt 11:28-30)

"The Lord is my portion," said my soul. Because of this, I will hope in him. The Lord is good to those who wait on him, to the soul that seeks him. It is good to stand ready in silence for the salvation of God. (Lam 3:25-26)

I will cry out, like a young swallow. I will moan, like a dove. My eyes have been weary by gazing upward. O Lord, I am oppressed! Be my security. (Is 38:14-15)

Strife, Quarrel, Fights

Refrain from strife, and you will diminish your sins. For an ill-tempered man enflames conflict, and a sinful man troubles his friends, and he casts hostility into the midst of those who have peace. (Sir 28:8-9)

Suffering

What are the blessings we receive when we accept our sufferings from God?

Suffering helps us overcome sin

Since Christ has suffered in the flesh, you also should be armed with the same intention. For he who suffers in the flesh desists from sin, so that now he may live, for the remainder of his time in the flesh, not by the desires of men, but by the will of God. (1 Pet 4:1-2)

Suffering is for our good

We know that all things work together unto good, for those who love God, who are called in accordance with his purpose. (Rom 8:28)

Suffering builds character

We also boast in our sufferings, knowing that suffering produces endurance, and endurance produces character, and character produces hope, and hope does not disappoint us. (Rom 5:3-5, NRSVCE)

We do not lose heart. Even though our outer nature is wasting away, our inner nature is being renewed day by day. (2 Cor 4:16, NRSVCE)

Suffering draws us closer to spiritual activities (such as reading the Bible)

Before I was humbled, I committed offenses; because of this, I have kept to your word. (Ps 119:67)

It is good for me that you humbled me, so that I may learn your statutes. (Ps 119:71)

Suffering helps us to become humble

Remember the entire journey along which the Lord your God led you, for forty years through the desert, in order to humble you, and to test you to make known the things that were in your heart, whether or not you would keep his commandments. (Deut 8:2)

Suffering prepares us for ministry (to serve God)

Blessed be the God and Father of our Lord Jesus Christ, the Father of mercies and the God of all consolation. He consoles us in all our tribulation, so that we too may be able to console those who are in any kind of distress, through the exhortation by which we also are being exhorted by God. (2 Cor 1:3-4)

If we are in tribulation, it is for your exhortation and salvation, or if we are in consolation, it is for your consolation, or if we are exhorted, it is for your exhortation and salvation, which results in the patient endurance of the same passion which we also endure. (2 Cor 1:6)

Souls can be saved by our sufferings

Do not be ashamed of the testimony of our Lord, nor of me, his prisoner. Instead, join with me in suffering for the Gospel with the strength that comes from God, who has freed us and has called us to his holy vocation, not according to our works, but according to his own purpose and grace, which was given to us in Christ Jesus, before the ages began. (2 Tim 1:8-9)

Suffering prepares us for spiritual warfare (makes us strong to face the enemy)

Blessed is the Lord, my God, who trains my hands for the battle and my fingers for the war. My rock and my fortress, my stronghold and my deliverer, my protector and him in whom I have hoped: he subdues my people under me. (Ps 144:1-2)

Suffering cleanses us from evil that is deep within us

The bruise of a wound, as well as scourges, shall wipe away evils in the more secret places of the inner self. (Pro 20:30)

Suffering helps us grow in the fruits of the Holy Spirit (e.g.: patience)

Let us examine him with insult and torture, that we may know his reverence and try his patience. Let us condemn him to a most shameful death, for, according to his own words, God will care for him. (Wis 2:19)

Christian suffering will make us more and more like Jesus

We ever carry around the mortification of Jesus in our bodies, so that the life of Jesus may also be manifested in our bodies. For we who live are ever handed over unto death for the sake of Jesus, so that the life of Jesus may also be manifested in our mortal flesh. (2 Cor 4:10-11)

Christian suffering is meant to make us perfect

It was fitting for him, because of whom and through whom all things exist, who had led many children into glory, should make the pioneer of their salvation perfect through sufferings. (Heb 2:10)

Although, certainly, he is the Son of God, he learned obedience by the things that he suffered. And having reached perfection, he was made, for all who are obedient to him, the cause of eternal salvation. (Heb 5:8-9)

Christian Suffering is a sign of God's presence
We are afflicted in every way, but not crushed; perplexed, but not driven to despair; persecuted, but not forsaken; struck down, but not destroyed; always carrying in the body the death of Jesus, so that the life of Jesus may also be made visible in our bodies. (2 Cor 4:8-10, NRSVCE)

If one of you suffers for being a Christian, he should not be ashamed. Instead, he should glorify God because he bears his name. (1 Pet 4:16)

It is better to suffer for doing good, if it is the will of God, than for doing evil. (1 Pet 3:17)

Though the Lord may give you the bread of adversity, and the water of affliction, yet your teacher will not hide from you anymore. And your eyes will behold your teacher. (Is 30:20)

Christian suffering is a sign that the Holy Spirit is resting on us
If you are reproached for the name of Christ, you will be blessed, because the Spirit of glory, which is the Spirit of God, rests upon you. (1 Pet 4:14)

Suffering is God's way of disciplining us
Persevere in discipline. God is treating you as children. But what child is there, whom his father does not correct? But if you are without that discipline in which all have become sharers, then you are illegitimate, and you are not his children. (Heb 12:7-8)

Christian suffering makes us strong (mature)
My brothers, when you have fallen into various trials, consider everything a joy, knowing that the testing of your faith produces endurance, and endurance brings a work to perfection, so that you may be mature and whole, deficient in nothing.(Jas 1:2-4)

Sufferings have a heavenly (eternal) reward

I consider that the sufferings of this time are not worthy to be compared with that future glory which shall be revealed in us. (Rom 8:18)

For though our affliction is, at the present time, temporary and light, it accomplishes in us the weight of a sublime eternal glory, beyond measure. And we are looking at, not the things that are seen, but the things that are unseen. For the things that are seen are temporary, whereas the things that are not seen are eternal. (2 Cor 4:17-18)

The God of all grace, who has called us to his eternal glory in Christ Jesus, will himself perfect, confirm, and establish us, after a brief time of suffering. (1 Pet 5:10)

For it is a credit to you if, being aware of God, you endure pain while suffering unjustly. (1 Pet 2:19, NRSVCE)

Blessed are they that suffer persecution for justice' sake: for theirs is the kingdom of heaven. Blessed are you when they shall revile you, and persecute you, and speak all that is evil against you, untruly, for my sake: Be glad and rejoice, for your reward is very great in heaven. (Matt 5:10-12, DRA)

Our Sufferings will add onto the sufferings of Christ and help in the salvation of the world

Most beloved, do not be surprised in the fiery trial taking place among you to test you, as though some strange thing is happening to you. But instead, be glad that you are sharing in the sufferings of Christ, that, when his glory will be revealed, you too may rejoice with exultation. (1 Pet 4:12-13)

Superstition

Do not be led away by changing or strange doctrines. And it is best for the heart to be sustained by grace, not by foods. For the latter have not been as useful to those who walked by them. (Heb 13:9)

Be rooted and continually built up in Christ. And be confirmed in the faith, just as you have also learned it, increasing in him with acts of thanksgiving. See to it that no one deceives you through philosophy and empty falsehoods, as found in the traditions of men, in accord with the influences of the world, and not in accord with Christ. (Col 2:7-8)

Prayer
Could any of the graven images of the Gentiles send rain? Or are the heavens able to give showers? Have we not hoped in you, the Lord our God? For you have made all these things. (Jer 14:22)

Suicidal tendencies

Prayer to overcome suicidal tendencies
To you, O Lord, I cried, and to the Lord I made supplication: "What profit is there in my death, if I go down to the Pit? Will the dust praise you? Will it tell of your faithfulness? Hear, O Lord, and be gracious to me! O Lord, be my helper!" (Ps 30:8-10, NRSVCE)

Word to meditate during suicidal thoughts
I shall not die, but live, and declare the works of the Lord. (Ps 118:17)

Surrender

Prayer of surrender
My Father, if it is possible, let this chalice pass away from me. Yet truly, let it not be as I will, but as you will. (Matt 26:39)

Into your hand I commit my spirit; you have redeemed me, O Lord, faithful God. (Ps 31:5, NRSVCE)

Behold, I am the handmaid of the Lord. Let it be done to me according to your word. (Luk 1:38)

Swearing

A man who swears many oaths will be filled with iniquity, and scourges will not depart from his house. And if he fails to fulfill it, his offense will be over him, and if he pretends he fulfilled it, he offends doubly. And if he swears an oath insincerely, he will not be justified. For his house will be filled with retribution for him. (Sir 23:11)

Before all things, my brothers, do not choose to swear, neither by heaven, nor by the earth, nor in any other oath. But let your word 'Yes' be yes, and your word 'No' be no, so that you may not fall under judgment. (Jas 5:12)

T

Talents (Natural gifts)

Whether you eat or drink, or whatever else you may do, do everything for the glory of God. (1 Cor 10:31)

Every excellent gift and every perfect gift is from above, descending from the Father of lights, with whom there is no change, nor any shadow of alteration. (Jas 1:17)

Tattoos and body piercings

You shall not cut your flesh for the dead, and you shall not make other figures or marks on yourself. I am the Lord. (Lev 19:28)

Tears

God's promise for those who are in tears
Bitterly, you will not weep. Mercifully, he will take pity on you. At the voice of your outcry, as soon as he hears, he will respond to you. (Is 30:19)

Temptations

God's promise for those going through temptations
No temptation has overtaken you such as is not common to everyone: but God is faithful, who will not let you be tested beyond what you are able; but with the temptation he will also make a way to escape, so that you may be able to endure it. (1 Cor 10:13)

Blessed is the man who suffers temptation. For when he has been proven, he shall receive the crown of life which God has promised to those who love him. (Jas 1:12)

Whosoever considers himself to be standing, let him be careful not to fall. (1 Cor 10:12)

For we do not have a high priest who is unable to have compassion on our weaknesses, but rather one who was tempted in all things, just as we are, yet without sin. Therefore, let us go forth with confidence toward the throne of grace, so that we may obtain mercy, and find grace, in a time of need. (Heb 4:15-16)

For in as much as he himself has suffered and has been tempted, he also is able to help those who are tempted. (Heb 2:18)

Thanksgiving

Thanksgiving prayer for the Gift of life

It was you who formed my inward parts; you knit me together in my mother's womb. (Ps 139:13)

My frame, which you have made in secret, has not been hidden from you, and my substance is woven in the lower parts of the earth. Your eyes saw my unformed substance, and in your book were written all the days that were formed for me, when none of it existed yet. (Ps 139:15-16)

You are the one who has drawn me out of the womb, my hope from the breasts of my mother. I have been thrown upon you from the womb; from the womb of my mother, you are my God. (Ps 22:9-10)

Thanksgiving prayer after surgery or healing from any sickness
O Lord my God, I cried to you for help, and you have healed me.
O Lord, you brought up my soul from Sheol, restored me to life from
among those gone down to the Pit. (Ps 30:1-2)

Thanksgiving prayer for protection and help
I will give thanks to you, O Lord, O King, and I will praise you, O
God my Savior. I will give thanks to your name: for you have been
a helper and protector to me. (Sir 51:1-2)

Thanksgiving prayer for success and victory
Lord, you will give us peace. For all our works have been done for
us by you. (Is 26:12)

Thanksgiving prayer after a miracle or blessing
Father, I thank you that you have heard me. And I know that you
hear me always: (Jn 11:41-42)

Thanksgiving prayer for spiritual gifts
To you, God of our ancestors, I give thanks, and you, I praise. For
you have given wisdom and fortitude to me, and now you have
revealed to me what we asked of you. (Dan 2:23)

Thanksgiving prayer of Daniel
May the name of the Lord be blessed by the present generation and
forever; for wisdom and fortitude are his. And he changes the times
and the ages. He takes away kingdoms and he establishes them. He
gives wisdom to those who are wise and teaching skills to those who
understand. He reveals deep and hidden things, and he knows what
has been established in darkness. And the light is with him. To you,
God of our ancestors, I give thanks, and you, I praise. For you have
given wisdom and fortitude to me, and now you have revealed to
me what we asked of you. (Dan 2:20-23)

Thanksgiving prayer for God's blessings

Bless the Lord, O my soul, and bless his holy name, all that is within me. Bless the Lord, O my soul, and do not forget all his recompenses. He forgives all your iniquities. He heals all your infirmities. He redeems your life from destruction. He crowns you with steadfast love and compassion. He satisfies your desire with good things. Your youth will be renewed like that of the eagle. (Ps 103:1-5)

Thanksgiving prayer for God's love

I will give thanks to you, O Lord my God, with my whole heart. And I will glorify your name in eternity. For your steadfast love toward me is great, and you have rescued my soul from the lower part of Hell. (Ps 86:12-13)

O give thanks to the Lord, for he is good, for his steadfast love endures forever. O give thanks to the God of gods, for his steadfast love endures forever. O give thanks to the Lord of lords, for his steadfast love endures forever. (Ps 136:1-3, NRSVCE)

Thanksgiving prayer for all the family blessings

Who am I, O Lord God, and what is my house, that you would grant such things to me? But even this has seemed little in your sight, and therefore you have also spoken about the house of your servant even for the future. And you have made me as someone of high rank, above all men, O Lord God. (1 Chron 17:16-17)

Thanksgiving prayer for God's mercy

I will give thanks to you, O Lord, because you have been angry with me; but your anger has been turned away, and you have consoled me. (Is 12:1)

What are the blessings we receive when we are thankful to God?

God's intervention in impossible situations

They took away the stone. Then, lifting up his eyes, Jesus said: "Father, I give thanks to you because you have heard me. And I know that you always hear me, but I have said this for the sake of the people who are standing nearby, so that they may believe that you have sent me." (Jn 11:41-42)

God performs signs and miracles

The men, in number about five thousand, sat down to eat. Therefore, Jesus took the bread, and when he had given thanks, he distributed it to those who were sitting down to eat; similarly also, from the fish, as much as they wanted. (Jn 6:10-11)

Our prayers will be answered when we are thankful to God

I will praise your name unceasingly, and I will praise it with thanksgiving, for my prayer was heeded. And you freed me from perdition, and you rescued me from the time of iniquity. (Sir 51:11)

We will be filled with God's presence

Enter his gates with thanksgiving, his courts with praise, and acknowledge him. Bless his name. (Ps 100:4)

Thoughts

Verse to meditate for those who are distracted

You will keep him in perfect peace, whose mind is stayed on you: because he trusts in you. (Is 26:2)

Verse to meditate for those with worldly and ungodly thoughts

Whatever is true, whatever is chaste, whatever is just, whatever is holy, whatever is worthy to be loved, whatever is of good repute, if there is any virtue, if there is any praiseworthy discipline: meditate on these. (Phil 4:8)

The peace of God, which exceeds all understanding, shall keep your hearts and minds through Christ Jesus. (Phil 4:7)

My thoughts are not your thoughts, and your ways are not my ways, says the Lord. For just as the heavens are exalted above the earth, so also are my ways exalted above your ways, and my thoughts above your thoughts. (Is 55:8-9)

Time

God's word about how to use time wisely
See to it that you live carefully, not like the foolish, but like the wise: making the most of the time, because the days are evil. (Eph 5:15-16)

Whoever works his land shall be satisfied with bread. But whoever pursues leisure will be filled with need. (Pro 28:19)

Tithing

What are the blessings we receive when we tithe?
Tithing brings financial blessings
Bring all the tithes into the storehouse, and let there be food in my house. And test me about this, says the Lord, as to whether I will not open to you the floodgates of heaven, and pour out to you a blessing, all the way to abundance. And I will rebuke for your sakes the devourer, and he will not corrupt the fruit of your land. Neither will the vine in the field be barren, says the Lord of hosts. (Mal 3:10-11)

You have looked for more, and behold, it became less, and you brought it home, and I blew it away. What is the cause of this, says the Lord of hosts? It is because my house is desolate, yet you have hurried, each one to his own house. Because of this, the heavens over you have been prohibited from giving dew, and the earth has been prohibited from giving her sprouts. (Hag 1:9-10)

Honor the Lord with your substance, and give to him from the first of all your fruits, and then your storehouses will be filled with abundance, and your presses shall overflow with wine. (Pro 3:9-10)

God keeps a count of our tithing and sacrifice for his kingdom
God is not unjust, such that he would forget your work and the love that you have shown in his name. For you have ministered, and you continue to minister, to the saints. (Heb 6:10)

Whoever receives a prophet, in the name of a prophet, shall receive the reward of a prophet. And whoever receives the just in the name of the just shall receive the reward of the just. And whoever shall give, even to one of the least of these, a cup of cold water to drink, solely in the name of a disciple: Amen I say to you, he shall not lose his reward. (Matt 10:41-42)

Prayer when offering a tithe
Who am I, and what is my people, that we should be able to make this offering to you? All is yours, and so the things that we received from your hand, we have given to you. (1 Chron 29:14)

I know, my God, that you test hearts, and that you love uprightness. Therefore, in the uprightness of my heart, I also have offered all these things willingly. (1 Chron 29:17)

Tiredness (Weariness)
Word to meditate
I have satiated the weary soul, and I have replenished all who are faint. Therefore I awoke, and beheld; and my sleep was pleasant unto me. (Jer 31:25-26)

He gives power to the weary, and strengthens the powerless. (Is 40:29)

Trauma, Misfortune

Word to meditate

In a day of good things, you should not be forgetful of misfortunes. And in a day of misfortunes, you should not be forgetful of good things. (Sir 11:25)

Travel and Journey

God's promise of protection for those who are travelling

The Lord will go before you. He will himself be with you. He will neither renounce nor abandon you. Do not be afraid, and do not dread. (Deut 31:8)

God's promise of Angelic protection for our journey

Behold, I will send my Angel, who will go before you, and preserve you on your journey, and lead you into the place that I have prepared. (Exo 23:20)

Trust in God

What are the blessings we receive for trusting in God?

Many are the torments of the wicked, but steadfast love surrounds those who trust in the Lord. (Ps 32:10, NRSVCE)

You keep him in perfect peace, whose mind stays on you: because he trusts in you. (Is 26:3)

May they trust in you, who know your name. For you have not abandoned those seeking you, Lord. (Ps 9:10)

Trust in the Lord with all your heart, and do not depend upon your own insight. In all your ways, acknowledge him, and he himself will direct your steps. (Pro 3:5-6)

Blessed is the man who trusts in the Lord, for the Lord will be his confidence. And he will be like a tree planted beside waters, which sends out its roots to moist soil. And it will not fear when the heat arrives. And its leaves will be green. And in the time of drought, it will not be anxious, nor will it cease at any time to bear fruit. (Jer 17:7-8)

A greedy man stirs up strife, but the one who trusts in the Lord will be enriched. (Ps 28:25)

In you our ancestors trusted; they trusted, and you delivered them. To you they cried, and were saved; in you they trusted, and were not put to shame. (Ps 22:4-5, NRSVCE)

Behold God is my savior, I will trust, and I will not be afraid. For the Lord is my strength and my praise, and he has become my salvation. (Is 12:2)

Trust in wealth

God's advice for those who trust in wealth
Whoever trusts in his riches will fall. But the just shall spring up like a green leaf. (Pro 11:28)

Do not choose to rely on your wealth, and you should not say: "I have all I need in life." (Sir 5:1)

Instruct the wealthy of this age not to have a superior attitude, nor to hope in the uncertainty of riches, but in the living God, who offers us everything in abundance to enjoy. (1 Tim 6:17)

The wealth of the rich is the city of his strength, and it is like a strong wall encircling him. (Pro 18:11)

Trials, Troubles, Tribulations

Do not let your hearts be troubled. You believe in God. Believe in me also. (Jn 14:1)

Our God is our refuge and strength, a helper in the tribulations that have greatly overwhelmed us. (Ps 46:1)

If I wander into the midst of tribulation, you will revive me. For you extended your hand against the wrath of my enemies. And your right hand has accomplished my salvation. (Ps 138:7)

When the righteous cry for help, the Lord hears, and rescues them from all their troubles. (Ps 34:17, NRSVCE)

Truth

If you will abide in my word, you will truly be my disciples. And you shall know the truth, and the truth shall set you free. (Jn 8:31-32)

I am the Way, and the Truth, and the Life. No one comes to the Father, except through me. (Jn 14:6)

U

Unbelief

Unbelief is an obstacle to God's blessings
He did not work many miracles there, because of their unbelief. (Matt 13:58)

He was not able to perform any miracles there, except that he cured a few of the infirm by laying his hands on them. And he wondered, because of their unbelief, (Mrk 6:5-6)

Prayer over somebody who is struggling with unbelief
O Lord, open his eyes, so that he may see. (2 Kgs 6:17)

Unemployment

God's promise for those who are unemployed
The Lord will guide you continually, and he will satisfy your soul in drought, and he will make strong your bones, and you will be like a watered garden and like a fountain of water whose waters will not fail. (Is 58:11)

Understanding

Prayer for the gift of understanding
Your hands have created me and formed me. Give me understanding, and I will learn your commandments. (Ps 119:73)

V

Victory

God's promise of victory for us

The Lord your God is the strength in your midst; a warrior who gives victory. He will rejoice over you with gladness. In his love, he will renew you. He will exult over you with praise. (Zeph 3:17)

Prayer for victory and success

O Lord, grant salvation to me. O Lord, grant us success. (Ps 118:25)

Vocation

Let each one lead the life just as the Lord has assigned to him, each one just as God has called him. (1 Cor 7:17)

Be all the more eager, so that by good works you may confirm your calling and election. For in doing these things, you do not sin at any time. (2 Pet 1:10)

W

Wait on God

God's promise for those who wait on him patiently
Wait for the Lord, and keep to his way. And he will exalt you, so as to inherit the land that you may seize. (Ps 37:34)

The Lord waits, so that he may take pity on you. And therefore, he will rise up to show mercy on you. For the Lord is the God of judgment. Blessed are all those who wait for him. (Is 30:18)

"The Lord is my portion," said my soul. Because of this, I will hope in him. The Lord is good to those who wait on him, to the soul that seeks him. It is good to stand ready in silence for the salvation of God. (Lam 3:25-26)

I will look towards the Lord. I will wait for God, my Savior. My God will hear me. (Mic 7:7)

Prayer to make while waiting on God
O Lord, take pity on us. For we have waited for you. Be our arm in the morning and our salvation in the time of trouble. (Is 33:2)

What are the blessings we receive when we wait on God?
We will see the greater glory of God
Upon hearing this, Jesus said to them: "This sickness is not unto death, but for the glory of God, so that the Son of God may be glorified by it." (Jn 11:4)

From ages past, no one has heard it, and they have not perceived it with the ears. Apart from you, O God, the eye has not seen what you have prepared for those who wait for you. (Is 64:4)

We will grow in faith
In the Promise of God, he did not waver out of distrust, but instead he was strengthened in faith, giving glory to God, knowing most fully that whatever God has promised, he is also able to accomplish. (Rom 4:20-21)

We will grow in patience
Yet we desire that each one of you display the same solicitude toward the fulfillment of hope, even unto the end, so that you may not be slow to act, but instead may be imitators of those who, through faith and patience, shall inherit the promises. (Heb 6:11-12)

We will grow strong in the Lord
Even the youth will faint and be weary, and young men will utterly fall. But they that wait on the Lord shall renew their strength. They will mount up with wings like eagles. They will run and not be weary. They will walk and not faint. (Is 40:30-31)

We will grow in joy
Behold, this is our God! We have waited for him, and he will save us. This is the Lord! We have endured for him. We will exult and rejoice in his salvation. (Is 25:9)

We will see God's work when we wait on him
From ages past, they have not heard it, and they have not perceived it with the ears. Apart from you, O God, the eye has not seen what you have prepared for those who wait for you. (Is 64:4)

Weakness

God's promise for those who are weak

My grace is sufficient for you. For power is perfected in weakness. (2 Cor 12:9-10)

Word to claim in times of weaknesses

I am content with weaknesses, in reproaches, in difficulties, in persecutions, in distresses, for the sake of Christ. For when I am weak, then I am strong. (2 Cor 12:10)

He is not weak with you, but is powerful with you. For although he was crucified in weakness, yet he lives by the power of God. And yes, we are weak in him. But we shall live with him by the power of God among you. (2 Cor 13:3-4)

My flesh and my heart may fail: but God is the strength of my heart, and my portion for ever. (Ps 73:26)

We do not have a high priest who is unable to have compassion on our weaknesses, but rather one who was tempted in all things, just as we are, yet without sin. Therefore, let us go forth with confidence toward the throne of grace, so that we may obtain mercy, and find grace, in a time of need. (Heb 4:15-16)

May you be made strong with all the strength that comes from his glorious power, and may you be prepared to endure everything with patience, while joyfully giving thanks to the Father, who has enabled you to share in the inheritance of the saints in the light. (Col 1:11-12, NRSVCE)

I shall be glorious in the eyes of the Lord, and my God shall be my strength. (Is 49:5)

Widow

God's hope for widows

Do not be afraid! For you will not be ashamed. Do not be discouraged, for you will not be put to disgrace. You shall forget the confusion of your youth, and you shall no longer remember the disgrace of your widowhood. (Is 54:4)

The Lord preserves the strangers; he upholds the orphan and the widow. (Ps 146:9)

Wife

God's advice to the wives

A loyal wife delights her husband, and she will fill up the years of his life with peace. (Sir 26:2)

I want you to know that the head of every man is Christ. But the head of woman is man. Yet truly, the head of Christ is God. (1 Cor 11:3)

A good wife is a great blessing. She will be given among the blessings of those who fear God, like a man who has done good deeds.(Sir 26:3)

Who shall find a capable wife? Far away, and from the furthest parts, is her price. The heart of her husband trusts in her, and he will not be deprived of spoils. She will repay him with good, and not evil, all the days of her life. She has sought wool and flax, and she has worked these by the counsel of her hands. She has become like a merchant's ship, bringing her bread from far away. And she has risen in the night, and given food to her household, and tasks to her maids. (Pro 31:10-15)

Wives, accept the authority of your husbands, so that, even if some do not believe the Word, they may be won over without the Word, through the behavior of their wives, as they see your reverence and your chaste behavior. (1 Pet 3:1-2)

There should be no unnecessary adornment of the hair, or surrounding with gold, or the wearing of ornate clothing. Instead, you should be a hidden person of the heart, with the incorruptibility of a quiet and meek spirit, rich in the sight of God. For in this way, in past times also, holy women adorned themselves, hoping in God, by accepting the authority of their husbands. (1 Pet 3:3-5)

A husband should fulfill his obligation to his wife, and a wife should also act similarly toward her husband. (1 Cor 7:3)

It is not the wife, but the husband, who has power over her body. But, similarly also, it is not the husband, but the wife, who has power over his body. (1 Cor 7:4)

Do not fail in your obligations to one another, except perhaps by consent, for a limited time, so that you may empty yourselves for prayer. And then, return together again, lest Satan tempt you by means of your abstinence. (1 Cor 7:5)

Wives should be submissive to their husbands, as to the Lord. For the husband is the head of the wife, just as Christ is the head of the Church. He is the Savior of his body. Therefore, just as the Church is subject to Christ, so also should wives be subject to their husbands in all things. (Eph 5:22-24)

A diligent woman is a crown to her husband. And she who brings shame is like decay to his bones. (Pro 12:4)

I want you to know that the head of every man is Christ. But the head of woman is man. Yet truly, the head of Christ is God. (1 Cor 11:3)

A wise woman builds up her household. But a foolish one will pull down with her own hands what has been built up. (Pro 14:1)

Will (Freewill, Choice)

God's Word about our freewill
Behold, I stand at the door and knock. If anyone will hear my voice and will open the door to me, I will enter to him, and I will dine with him, and he with me. (Rev 3:20)

Thus says the Lord: Behold, I set before you the way of life and the way of death. (Jer 21:8)

Consider what I have set forth in your sight this day, life and good, or, on the opposite side, death and evil. (Deut 30:15)

I call heaven and earth as witnesses this day, that I have set before you life and death, blessing and curse. Therefore, choose life, so that both you and your offspring may live. (Deut 30:19)

Word to meditate for those who have a weak will power
If you will abide in my word, you will truly be my disciples. And you shall know the truth, and the truth shall set you free. (Jn 8:31-32)

Now the Spirit is Lord. And wherever the Spirit of the Lord is, there is liberty. (2 Cor 3:17)

Will of God

What are the blessings we receive when we do the will of God?

We enter the kingdom of God

Not all who say to me, 'Lord, Lord,' will enter into the kingdom of heaven. But whoever does the will of my Father, who is in heaven, the same shall enter into the kingdom of heaven. (Matt 7:21)

We gain eternal life

The world is passing away, with its desire. But whoever does the will of God abides unto eternity. (1 Jn 2:17)

We become part of God's family

Anyone who does the will of my Father, who is in heaven is my brother, and sister, and mother. (Matt 12:50)

Prayer to seek the will of God

My Father, if it is possible, let this cup pass away from me. Yet truly, let it not be as I will, but as you will. (Matt 26:39)

God's promise when we pray according to his will

This is the boldness which we have toward God that if we ask anything according to his will, he hears us. (1 Jn 5:14)

Wisdom

God's promise to those who seek wisdom

If anyone among you is in need of wisdom, let him ask God, who gives abundantly to all without reproach, and it shall be given to him. (Jas 1:5)

What are the blessings of divine wisdom?

Godly wisdom will help us know and understand spiritual matters
We assess with difficulty the things that are of earth, and we discover with labor the things that are within our view. So who will search out the things that are in heaven? Moreover, who will know your mind, unless you give wisdom and send your Holy Spirit from on high? (Wis 9:16-17)

Godly wisdom influences our thinking and speech
My son, pay attention to my wisdom, and incline your ear to my prudence, so that you may guard your thinking, and so that your lips may preserve discipline. (Pro 5:1-2)

Godly Wisdom can help us understand the natural world around us
He has given me true knowledge of these things which exist: so as to know the orderly arrangement of the world, and the powers of the elements, the beginning and the end and the midpoint of the seasons, the characteristics of changing things, and the divisions of time, the courses of the years, and the orderly arrangement of the stars, the natures of animals, and the rage of wild beasts, the force of winds, and the reasonings of men, the diversities of plants, and the benefits of roots, and all such things as are hidden and unexpected, I have learned; for wisdom, the artisan of all things, taught me. (Wis 7:17-21)

Godly wisdom leads to other blessings in life
All good things came to me together with her, and innumerable wealth by her hand; and I rejoiced in all these, because wisdom leads them. (Wis 7:11)

Wisdom protects us from sin (helps us to avoid sin)
Say to wisdom, "You are my sister," and call prudence your friend. So may she guard you from the woman who is an outsider, and from the stranger who sweetens her words. (Pro 7:4-5)

Work

Prayer to lift up persecution at work
You are my strength and my refuge; and for the sake of your name, you will lead me and nourish me. You will lead me out of this snare, which they have hidden for me. For you are my protector. (Ps 31:3-4)

God's promise for people who are not appreciated for their work
Let your voice cease from crying and your eyes from tears. For there is a reward for your work, says the Lord. (Jer 31:16)

God's advice about our attitude toward work
Whatever your task, do it from the heart, as done for the Lord, and not for men. (Col 3:23)

Works (Good works)

What are the blessings of good works?
There is a reward for good works
And so, let us not grow weary in doing good. For in due time, we shall reap without fail. (Gal 6:9)

Our Good works will be remembered at the time of final judgment
Amen I say to you, whenever you did this for one of these, the least of my brothers, you did it for me. (Matt 25:40)

We will be judged based on our works
For it is necessary for us to appear before the judgment seat of Christ, so that each one may receive recompense for what has been done in the, whether it was good or evil. (2 Cor 5:10)

Behold, I am approaching quickly! And my repayment is with me, to render to each one according to his works. (Rev 22:12)

Workers

God's promise for workers
The Lord will send forth a blessing upon your cellars, and upon all the works of your hands. And he will bless you in the land that you shall receive. (Deut 28:8)

Worldliness

God's advice and warning to those who are worldly
Do not choose to love the world, nor the things that are in the world. If anyone loves the world, the love of the Father is not in him. For all that is in the world-the desire of the flesh, and the desire of the eyes, and the pride of life-is not of the Father, but is of the world. (1 Jn 2:15-16)

Do not choose to store up for yourselves treasures on earth: where rust and moth consume, and where thieves break in and steal. Instead, store up for yourselves treasures in heaven: where neither rust nor moth consumes, and where thieves do not break in and steal. For where your treasure is, there also is your heart. (Matt 6:19-21)

If for this life only we have hoped in Christ, then we are most to be pitied than all people. (1 Cor 15:19)

Worry

God's promise for those who worry

Do not worry about your life, as to what you will eat, nor about your body, as to what you will wear. Is not life more than food, and the body more than clothing? Consider the birds of the air, how they neither sow, nor reap, nor gather into barns, and yet your heavenly Father feeds them. Are you not of much greater value than they are? (Matt 6:25-26)

Which of you, by worrying, is able to add single hour to your span of life? And why do you worry about clothing? Consider the lilies of the field, how they grow; they neither work nor weave. But I say to you, that not even Solomon, in all his glory, was clothed like one of these. So if God so clothes the grass of the field, which is here today, and cast into the oven tomorrow, how much more will clothe you, O little in faith? (Matt 6:27-30)

Can any of you by worrying add a single hour to your span of life? Therefore, if you are not capable, in what is so little, why do you worry about the rest? (Luk 12:25-26)

Worship

Prayer of worship

Great and marvelous are your works, Lord God Almighty; just and true are your ways, you King of the nations. Who shall not fear you, O Lord, and glorify your name? for you alone are holy: for all nations shall come and worship before you; for your judgments are made manifest. (Rev 15:3-4)

What are the blessings we receive when we worship God?

We will be blessed financially and with good health

You shall worship the Lord your God, so that I may bless your bread and your waters, and so that I may take away sickness from your midst. There will not be fruitless or barren ones in your land. I will fill up the number of your days. (Exo 23:25-26)

Worship of God will help us overcome sin

The worship of the one God sets man free from turning in on himself, from the slavery of sin and the idolatry of the world. (CCC 2097)

Worship of God brings deliverance from evil

Then it happened that, while Samuel was offering the burnt offering, the Philistines began the battle against Israel. But the Lord thundered with a great crash, on that day, over the Philistines, and he terrified them, and they were cut down before the face of Israel. (1 Sam 7:10)

Worship brings healing and restoration on the land (home, country)

In that place, David built an altar to the Lord. And he offered burnt offerings and peace offerings. And the Lord was gracious to the land, and the plague was held back from Israel. (2 Sam 24:25)

Worship brings blessings on our descendants

For in like manner as the new heavens and the new earth, which I will cause to stand before me, says the Lord, so will your offspring and your name stand. And there will be month after month, and Sabbath after Sabbath. And all flesh will approach, so as to worship before me, says the Lord. (Is 66:22-23)

Worthlessness

God's word of encouragement for those feeling worthless

Even the very hairs of your head have all been numbered. Therefore, do not be afraid. You are worth more than many sparrows. (Luk 12:7)

Because you are precious and honorable in my eyes, I have loved you, and I will present men on behalf of you, and nations on behalf of your life. (Is 43:4)

Consider the birds of the air, how they neither sow, nor reap, nor gather into barns, and yet your heavenly Father feeds them. Are you not of much greater value than they are? (Matt 6:25-26)

Y

Youth

God's promise for the youth who read and meditate on the Bible
How can young people keep their way pure? By keeping to your words. (Ps 119:9)

God's promise for the youth who are faced with various challenges
It is good for a man, to carry the yoke in his youth. He shall sit solitary and silent when the Lord has imposed it. He shall place his mouth in the dirt, perhaps there may be hope. (Lam 3:27-29)

Z

Zeal

God's promise for those who lack zeal (drive) to do anything
I have satiated the weary soul, and I have replenished all who are faint. (Jer 31:25)

It is he that gives power to the weary, and strengthens them that are powerless. Youths shall faint, and labor, and young men shall fall exhausted. But they that hope in the Lord shall renew their strength, they shall take wings as eagles, they shall run and not be weary, they shall walk and not faint. (Is 40:29-31)

Abbreviation

Gen-Genesis	Song-Song of Solomon	Jn-John
Exo-Exodus	Wis-Wisdom	Acts-Acts
Lev-Leviticus	Sir-Sirach	Rom-Romans
Num-Numbers	Is- Isaiah	1 Cor-1 Corinthians
Deut-Deuteronomy	Jer-Jeremiah	2 Cor-2 Corinthians
Josh-Joshua	Lam-Lamentations	Gal-Galatians
Judg-Judges	Bar-Baruch	Eph-Ephesians
Ruth-Ruth	Eze-Ezekiel	Phil-Philippians
1 Sam-1 Samuel	Dan-Daniel	Col-Colossians
2 Sam-2 Samuel	Hos-Hosea	Tit-Titus
1 Kgs-1 Kings	Joel-Joel	Phlm-Philemon
2 Kgs-2 Kings	Amos-Amos	1 Thes-1 Thessalonians
1 Chron-1 Chronicles	Obad-Obadiah	2 Thes-2 Thessalonians
2 Chron-2 Chronicles	Jon-Jonah	1 Tim- 1Timothy
Ezr-Ezra	Mic-Micah	2 Tim-2 Timothy
Neh-Nehemiah	Nah-Nahum	Heb-Hebrew
Tob-Tobith	Hab-Habakkuk	Jas-James
Judith-Judith	Zeph-Zephaniah	1 Pet-1 Peter
Est-Esther	Hag-Haggai	2 Pet-2 Peter
1 Mac-1 Maccabees	Zech-Zechariah	1 Jn- 1 John
2 Mac-2 Maccabees	Mal-Malachi	2 Jn- 2 John
Job-Job	Matt-Matthew	3 Jn- 3 John
Ps-Psalms	Mrk-Mark	Jude-Jude
Pro-Proverbs	Luk-Luke	Rev-Revelation
Eccl-Ecclesiastes		

Other Titles from Gifted Books and Media

RETURN TO GOD
Confession Handbook

PREACHER'S HANDBOOK

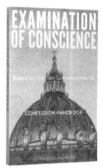

EXAMINATION OF CONSCIENCE

EUCHARISTIC ADORATION
Prayers, Devotions, and Meditations

EXAMINATION OF CONSCIENCE
For Children

EXAMINATION OF CONSCIENCE
For Teens

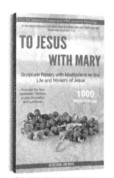

TO JESUS WITH MARY
*Scriptural Rosary on the Life and
Ministry of Jesus*

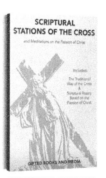

SCRIPTURAL STATIONS
OF THE CROSS

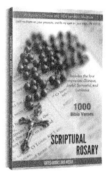

SCRIPTURAL ROSARY
1000 Bible Verses

Now on Sale
Available in Paperback and Ebook
www.giftedbookstore.com

Made in the USA
Middletown, DE
16 April 2023

28976069R00169